CHRIST AND BUDDHA

CHRIST AND BUDDHA

Josiah Nelson Cushing

Henry Melville king

GYAN

Published by

Gyan Publishing House
5, Ansari Road
Daryaganj, New Delhi-110002
Phone: 011-47034999, 9811692060
E-mail: books@gyanbooks.com

Distribution Network
gyanbooks.com
India, USA, Canada, UK, Australia, France

ISBN: 978-81-212-9428-7 (PB)
First Published, 1907

2nd Impression 2023

Printed at: Gyan Press, Delhi.

CHRIST AND BUDDHA

AUTHOR: Josiah Nelson Cushing, Henry Melville king

Christ and Buddha

Christ and Buddha

By

Josiah Nelson Cushing

D. D., Ph. D.

Missionary for Forty Years in Burma
Late President of the Rangoon College

With an Appreciation of the Author

By

Henry Melville King

Pastor Emeritus
of the First Baptist Church in Providence, R. I.

Published by the request and with the generous aid of friends

Philadelphia

American Baptist Publication Society

Boston Chicago Atlanta
New York St. Louis Dallas

Contents

An Appreciation

AMONG the many papers left by the late Dr. Josiah Nelson Cushing was found a manuscript which discusses in a candid, concise, yet comprehensive manner the contrast between Christianity and Buddhism. The manuscript was one of the latest productions of his pen, and evidently was regarded by him as complete, for he had signed his name at the end, and written the date and place of its completion. It was completed at Ceylon, the country where Buddhism can be observed and studied to the best advantage, both as a system of beliefs, unaffected by the Christian forces which have materially modified the Buddhism of India, Burma, and other lands, and also in its practical fruits in the lives and characters of its adherents.

This manuscript, evidently the result of long study and personal investigation, wide reading and discriminating comparison, was placed in my hands by Mrs. Cushing just before her return to Burma, in the autumn of 1905, to take up, so far as possible, certain lines of literary work left unfinished by her late honored husband. She expressed the wish that it might be carefully examined, and if found suitable, might be published as a fitting memorial of Doctor Cushing. I have called to my aid missionary secretaries, and missionaries competent to express a judgment as to its worth, and all to whom it has been submitted have pronounced the work to be one of great value, and calculated to win and instruct readers, who might be repelled by the larger and more elaborate works of Kuenen, Max Müller, Sir Monier Williams, Rhys Davids and others. It is believed that in addition to the "Cushing Memorial Hall" to be erected in connection with the Rangoon Baptist College, in the presidency of which Doctor Cushing spent the last years of his life, and other memorials on the field of his labors, a memorial volume would be welcomed not only abroad, but in the homeland by his many friends; and it is also believed that a brief biographical sketch and appreciation of Doctor Cushing by one who knew him from his student days, was his instructor in the Hebrew language, and enjoyed his lifelong friendship, would make the little volume doubly welcome.

Doctor Cushing was born in North Attleboro, Mass., May 4, 1840. He was the son of Alpheus Nelson and Charlotte E. Foster Cushing. He was prepared for college at the Pierce Academy, Middleboro, Mass., and entered Brown University in the class of 1862, in the same class with Dr. Henry F. Colby, of Dayton, Ohio, Rev. Addison Parker, of Piqua, Ohio, and Dr. Josiah R. Goddard, of Ningpo, China. After his graduation he went directly to Newton Theological Institution, completing the full course. Among his classmates there were Dr. Luther G. Barrett, the president of Jackson College, Jackson, Miss., and Dr. Alonzo Bunker, who also gave his life to missionary service, and was a successful missionary to the Karens at Toungoo and Loikaw, Burma, for forty years, laboring in the same country with Doctor Cushing and for the same period of time.

As to many another student, the obtaining of an education was to young Cushing a financial struggle. But he was dominated by a great purpose, and no obstacle was permitted to change or hinder it. In the theological seminary he is remembered as a student of delightful spirit, of gentlemanly deportment, of far more than average intellectual ability, and of complete consecration to the work to which he believed God had called him. Here was exhibited, as also in college, his remarkable linguistic ability, and here was ripened the definite purpose which ruled his life, to make known the glad tidings of Christ's salvation to the heathen world. The year before he completed his college course he united by letter with the First Baptist Church in Providence. After completing his seminary course he was ordained to the Christian ministry by the same church in 1865, and in its fellowship he died, though for a brief period he transferred his membership to the English-speaking church in Rangoon, of which for a time he filled the pastoral office, in addition to his other duties.

In 1865 he offered himself to the American Baptist Missionary Union as a candidate for the foreign field, and was presented at the annual meeting held that year in St. Louis, as a missionary under appointment, in the same city where, by a remarkable coincidence, after nearly forty years of successful labor, he was translated to his reward on high. He was retained at the seminary as instructor in the Hebrew department for one year, and in 1866 he sailed for Burma, being designated to the Shan tribes to take up a work which had been recently begun by Dr. Moses H. Bixby, but which he had been compelled to lay down by reason of failing health. These tribes were as yet little known, and in large part unreached by missionary operations. Doctor Cushing entered courageously into the difficult and dangerous task of visiting the people in their homes, and carrying to them the knowledge of the Christian religion, with Toungoo as his headquarters, extending his tours farther and farther into the wild and untraversed country inhabited by these people.

The Shans are sturdy mountaineers, and occupy the most eastern section of Burma, bordering on Siam and China. They are nominally Buddhists, and offer sacrifices to spirits, and are controlled by many inherited superstitions. Doctor Cushing studied the country, and studied the people, their customs and mode of life as well as their language. The knowledge thus gained, geographical and racial, was of great value to the English government, as it gratefully acknowledged. For ten years he continued this work of exploration and personal evangelization by frequent and extended tours from Toungoo, and then for three years he stationed himself at Bhamo, four hundred miles farther into the northeastern interior, beyond the utmost reach of civilization, and in the very center of the people whom he was seeking to enlighten and elevate.

But God had a special and important work for him to do, a work which he was peculiarly fitted by natural endowment and intellectual attainments to undertake, and for which his intimate acquaintance with the people had been preparing him. He found the people lacking the facilities of a written language, without which religion cannot become a permanent and enlightening force, and no high degree of civilization can be attained. He gave himself to the task of compiling a Shan dictionary, which he accomplished with immense labor. His residence was now changed to Rangoon, where he could have the needed assistance of the printing-press. In 1880 he published an "Elementary Handbook of the Shan Language," and also a "Grammatical Sketch of the Kachin Language," an allied language. The "Elementary Handbook" went to a second edition in 1888. The completed "Shan and English Dictionary" was issued in 1881. His next great work, that which had all the while been in his mind and in gradual preparation, was the translation of the sacred Scriptures into the Shan tongue. For this he was eminently qualified by his accurate knowledge of the Greek and Hebrew languages, and his linguistic genius. Upon it he spent many years of careful and conscientious study, publishing the word of God, book by book, first the New Testament and then the Old, the New Testament first appearing in 1882, and passing to a second edition in 1887, and to a third edition in 1903, at which time the whole Bible was ready to be put into the hands of the people, revised and perfected by himself. The Old Testament translation first appeared in 1891. This great achievement will stand as Doctor Cushing's imperishable monument, and places his name side by side with the names of Carey, Judson, Brown, and other translators of the word of God. He also prepared a Shan hymn book, and began the preparation of a literature for the people.

In 1893 Doctor Cushing was requested to assume the care of the Baptist College in Rangoon, an institution then small, but which under his wise and able leadership has grown to rank with the foremost educational institutions in Burma, having an enrolment at the present time of about eight hundred students in all departments. The college was founded for the benefit of all the races in Burma—Burmese, Sgau Karens, Pwo Karens, Shans, Kachins, etc. The office of president he held until his death, laboring to carry forward the school to the highest point of efficiency, and anxious to see it placed upon a permanent foundation in the possession of an adequate endowment. He was often urged to lay aside the burdens of administration, and give himself to the more quiet, but no less necessary work of the preparation of a larger religious literature for the people, he being the man most competent to do this. But the needs of the college were to him imperative.

One purpose of his last visit to this country was to assist in the appeal for an endowment of five hundred thousand dollars for the mission schools of the denomination. He had but recently reached America, in the early summer of 1905, and hastened to St. Louis to attend the annual meetings of the Baptist Missionary Societies, which occur in May. There, having received the happy greetings of his admiring friends, and looked once more into the faces of those who were fellow-workers with him and with God in the extension of his kingdom in the world, at the close of one of the public meetings on May 17, on the floor of the church where the meeting was held, he fell unconscious, and quickly breathed his last. In an instant of time, without warning, his spirit was translated into the presence of Him whom he had served with lifelong and conspicuous devotion, and into the undimmed light of the knowledge of the glory of God, which he had labored to disseminate in the dark places of the earth.

The sudden death of Doctor Cushing in circumstances so peculiar and impressive, made a profound impression upon those assembled at the meetings, and its announcement was received with deepest sorrow on two continents. To him the time of his going was most opportune, but his departure left the sense of an irreparable loss in a multitude of hearts. Public funeral services were held two days later in the same church from which his spirit took its flight, in which those who had known him and been associated with him paid tender and affectionate tribute to his high personal character, his rare attainments, and his conspicuous usefulness, in the presence of many fellow-missionaries and the leaders of the denomination, who constituted a remarkable and most sympathetic audience. Later his body was taken to Plymouth, Mass., for burial.

Doctor Cushing was a man of great refinement of taste, and of remarkable tact and courtesy of bearing, which fitted him to move in the highest educational and social circles. He won for the college a wide patronage, and for himself personally the confidence and favor of government officials, and the great respect of the representatives of other religious communions with whom he had to do. The government of India often committed to him missions of great importance and delicacy.

His attainments as a scholar were exceptional. He mastered not only the Shan language, in which he was an acknowledged authority, but the Burmese and the Kachin also, an unusual accomplishment, and was an expert student and successful teacher of Pali, the literary language of Buddhism. He was a representative abroad of American Christianity, of whom it could well be proud. He was honored by his Alma Mater, which conferred upon him the degree of Master of Arts in 1865, of Doctor of Divinity in 1881, and subsequently the degree of Doctor of Philosophy "in recognition of attainments" in 1898, an almost unparalleled occurrence.

His great ability and distinguished services were, if possible, still more highly recognized and honored by learned societies in England. He was elected a member of the Royal Asiatic Society, a Fellow of the Royal Geographical Society, a member of the Society of Arts, a Fellow of the Royal Meteorological Society, and a member of the Victoria Institute, all of London. He was also a member of the Educational Syndicate of Burma for seventeen years, and vice-president of that body for eight years by government appointment. Since 1886 he had been a member of the government Text Book Committee of India. There seemed to be no honor or position of high service within the gift of those who were acquainted with his character and achievements, of which he was not deemed worthy.

Before the adjournment of the anniversary meetings of the American Baptist Missionary Union in St. Louis, resolutions were adopted by that body in recognition of Doctor Cushing's conspicuous position as scholar, translator, educator, and Christian, and bearing grateful testimony to his prodigious learning, literary accomplishments, executive ability, impressive personality, sound judgment, and eminent service. The resolutions expressed the sincere and unanimous appreciation of the great Missionary Society which passed them, and as an official utterance are here preserved:

The recent startling event, the sudden death of Rev. Josiah N. Cushing, D. D., PH. D., one of our honored missionaries, while in attendance at this annual meeting of the Union, may well produce deep solemnity, and move us to an expression of our feeling in view of this mysterious providence, and of our high appreciation of the beloved and honored brother, whom God so suddenly called to himself.

Doctor Cushing was educated at Brown University and at the Newton Theological Institution. ..Called of God to the service of foreign missions, he applied for appointment as a missionary to Burma, and forty years ago, in this very city of St. Louis, was solemnly set apart to the work in the foreign field. These forty years were crowded full of missionary activity. As an evangelist, he announced the gospel message to multitudes who sat in darkness and in the shadow of death, won many souls, and brought them as trophies of grace to the feet of his Lord. As a translator, he gave to many thousands the Bible, the dictionary, the instructive tract, and an informing and healthful literature. As a traveler, he explored distant regions and opened hitherto unknown sections of the country to commerce and to religion. As an educator, he gathered around him the youth of the land, trained their minds and enriched them with the treasures of knowledge. He built up for their advantage a prosperous and promising college, and gave to the people a system of education whose value they were not slow to perceive. As a scholar, he acquainted himself, in an extensive degree, with general literature, both in his native and in foreign tongues. He mastered several Asiatic languages and spoke them with fluency and accuracy, and commanded high respect for his intellectual strength and mental attainments. As a preacher, he was faithful, earnest, and eloquent, and impressed his hearers with the strength of his thought and the fervor of his spirit. As a man, he was just and generous, charitable and sympathetic, of unquestioned integrity and superior judgment. His noble character was gladly recognized by his brethren, while his scientific investigations and his services to mankind secured just honors from institutions of learning. In his death the world loses one of its noblest men, and our Union one of its prominent and most successful missionaries. A useful man, a consecrated Christian, we deplore his death and revere his memory.

It was fitting that so noble and devoted a life should have a glorious termination. And it came within a few days after his return to his native land for needed rest and recuperation, in the company of his brethren, who loved and honored him. In a moment, in the twinkling of an eye, "he was not, for God took him." Swift was his translation, speedy his glorious coronation.

Our deep sympathy is extended to the bereaved wife and son, while we assure them of our fervent prayers that the God in whom the sainted husband and father so fully and so constantly trusted, and who is the God of all consolation, may give them comfort, sufficient and abiding.

The name of Dr. Josiah N. Cushing will stand high upon the roll of missionary worthies, who have given their lives to extend the knowledge and the kingdom of God in obedience to the final commission of his Son, Jesus Christ, and to carry to the degraded and unenlightened peoples of the earth the light and blessings of a Christian civilization and the hope of a Christian immortality. He was a fresh illustration of how God can use a man who puts himself unreservedly in his hands, and can make his influence for the good of mankind far-reaching and enduring. The story of his life and service is added to the rich treasure of missionary biography, which is the priceless possession of the whole Christian church. To the Baptist denomination the memory of his character and work will remain a source of grateful pride and perpetual inspiration. To those who have been permitted to know him from his student days, and in the intimacy of personal friendship, he will be cherished as a brother beloved. Well for him that he was translated with undiminished powers and at the height of his great usefulness.

Speak no more of his renown,
Lay your earthly fancies down;
In the solemn temple leave him,
God accept him. Christ receive him.

HENRY M. KING.

PROVIDENCE, R. I., January 1, 1907.

Christ and Buddha

A DEEP interest in Buddhism needs no apology on my part. For more than thirty years I have been brought into constant and intimate contact with it, not simply in the coast districts of Burma where foreign influences are distinctly felt, but in the distant interior where until very recently the foreigner had never come and the people held intact their ancestral beliefs. In the preparation of my Shan and English Dictionary it became necessary to examine extensively the literature of the Shans. This literature is largely a collection of Buddhist books, the most of which are translations from the Burmese language. I have always had the pleasure of the helpful acquaintance of a good number of Buddhist monks, well educated in the books of their faith, who were ready to give any information about their religion that was desired, and to discuss quietly,

Introductory

and as exhaustively as they were able, any points of doctrine difficult to understand. It was also my very good fortune to enjoy the friendship of the learned and scholarly Bishop Bigandet during the last twelve years of his eventful life. The extensive knowledge of Buddhism which he possessed is shown in his widely known "Life of Gautama." He was always ready to open his stores of information for the benefit of others, and I often availed myself of his kindness and personal friendship to gain light on obscure and difficult subjects. I ought not to forget to acknowledge the extremely valuable information that I gained from Dr. Emil Forchhammer, Professor of Pali in the Government College at Rangoon, and Government Archæologist, of whose family I was at one time a member. The results of his profound study of Buddhism and diligent investigation of ancient Buddhist monuments and inscriptions in Burma were largely lost to the world through his premature death. During the last five years my interest in Buddhism has been intensified by the study of Pali and of Sanskrit which has brought me into direct acquaintance with the original text of the Pitakas so far as they have been published. During the last three months I have been staying in Ceylon, and have improved the opportunity to investigate Buddhism in the island where Mahinda was the great first missionary, and where many of the monks thoroughly understand the tenets of their religion, although the common people, as in Burma, are much addicted to practising the worship of spirits, especially demons, while they conform outwardly to the customs of Buddhism.

There are other than personal reasons why the study of Buddhism is interesting. It is a religion which has been accepted for centuries, by many millions of the human race, and still, in its various phases, is spread over Ceylon, Burma, Siam, China, Korea, Japan, and Thibet. From Asoka's celebrated edicts inscribed on rocks and stone pillars, beginning about 250 B. C. and situated in places at immense distances from one another, we learn that Buddhism had already spread throughout his vast Indian empire and even in adjacent countries. Although it disappeared from India about the twelfth century, it has ever maintained a vast and molding influence in many other

Asiatic countries. Before Christianity arose, the adherents of Buddhism were very many, and it is doubtless true that it has, in its history, had more followers than Christianity or any other single religion. It is safe to say that at the present time no two religions exert a wider direct and indirect influence than Buddhism and Christianity, the one by its quiet, tenacious hold on a multitude of men, the other by its vigorous, aggressive life that not only leads its followers to an active religious effort, but seeks to attract men of other faiths to its acceptance. Once Buddhism had a missionary spirit as Christianity now has, and its dogmas, whatever we may think of them as a whole, had as winning a power over many new nations as it now has a keeping power over many old nations. The secret of that mighty power cannot fail to arouse the interest of a thoughtful mind.

Its voluminous literature appeals to the scholar as a vast thesaurus of Oriental thought, feeling, and aspiration. History, philosophy, ethics, poetry, myth, and song await the curious student. Amid much that is extravagant in fancy, or even childish in character, there are the profound thoughts of sages and the wrestlings of noble minds with the great questions that arise out of human being and life. Its Dhammapada has much in common with the wisdom of the Book of Proverbs. There are lyric songs in the Udāna, didactic poems in the Sulta Nipāta, a wealth of folk-lore in the Jātakas, and treatises, moral and metaphysical, in the Abhidhamma, and other parts of the Pitakas. To the student of human thought and to the investigator of comparative religion, this extensive literature is a mine of inestimable value.

I have sought to approach the consideration of Buddhism with a fair mind. Firmly convinced as I am of the truth of Christianity and of the fact that in Christianity we have the clear revelation of the mind and will of God, I desire to give full recognition to the many excellencies that exist in Buddhist teachings, and when compelled to condemn what I deem erroneous, to do so in as candid and impartial manner as possible. There is divine light in the non-Christian religions of the world. We are taught in the Bible that God has not left himself without a witness among all peoples, not only in the glorious works of creation, but in the law written on all human hearts (Rom. 1), that he is "No respecter of persons, but in every nation he that feareth him and worketh righteousness is acceptable to him."[1] In John's teaching concerning the Incarnation, Christ is held up as the Author of all things, for "All things were made by him and without him was not anything made that was made," and he is represented as the world's great Light-giver—"That was the true Light which lighteth every man that cometh into the world."

What is good in the teaching of the non-Christian religions are rays of the divine light reflected from human hearts upon which it shines, though often distorted and broken by the obscuring atmosphere of sin and superstition through which they pass. They are welcome proofs that God's revelation of himself apart from Christ still sheds some degree of light in all human souls. It is not strange, then, that in many things the moral code of Buddhism has much common ground with Christianity, and deserves recognition of its true value. To hold up what is false to public condemnation and

[1] Acts 10: 34, 35.

ignore the good which deserves praise is narrow-minded, unjust, and even fanatical. In passing I may properly remark that the Christian missionary who pursues this policy deprives himself of most valuable assistance in winning his way into Buddhists' minds by the frank acknowledgment of what every true-minded man must accept as good in their religion. That truth is an inestimably useful foundation on which to build up in men's minds the higher and more perfect truth of Christ.

Limitation of Subject

IN an essay like this, of necessarily limited length, there must inevitably be a less detailed treatment of many points of much interest, than in the larger space of a more comprehensive work. But I have endeavored to give prominence to what has seemed to be most important in the Buddhist system, as taught in the Hīna-yāna, Little Vehicle (sometimes called the Southern Vehicle), as distinguished from the Mahā-yāna, Great Vehicle (also called the Northern Vehicle). The Little Vehicle prevails in Ceylon, Burma, and Siam, and is undoubtedly much the purer form of Buddhism. The Great Vehicle has spread over China, Korea, Japan, is held by some Mongol tribes, and in its latest developments prevails as the religion of Thibet. It is a great expansion of the Little Vehicle, with many divergences of doctrine, often carried to such an extent that they antagonize the early teaching of Gotama, as in the theory of the Adi-Buddha and Dhyāni Buddhas. It differs greatly in each of the Northern countries, culminating in the Lamaism of Thibet with its mysticism and hierarchy. Moreover, in China it seems to share amicably a place with Confucianism and Taoism, and in Japan with Shintoism, in the hearts of its followers. While the Little Vehicle is an older and more genuine form of Buddhism, yet even it has never succeeded in driving out serpent worship, spirit worship, and other ancient cults which it sought to supplant, but has become mixed with them in the beliefs and practices of the common people. So true is this in Burma that the officer detailed as the compiler of the last census in that country, in his chapter on the Buddhist religion, took the position that animism, under a veneering Buddhism, was really the practical religion of the masses. Still it must be acknowledged that the people in Burma, Ceylon, and Siam do regard Buddhism as their faith, notwithstanding the power which demon worship and other local superstitions exert over them, and that many monks, and not a few of the laity, are devout students of the books of the Southern Vehicle.

Is Buddhism a Religion?

AT the outset the question arises whether Buddhism may be strictly called a religion. While we are accustomed to treat it as a religion, it lacks the important notes of a religion, and is really a system of philosophy of a pessimistic character. It has much moral teaching, but morality is not necessarily religion. If religion is derived from *religo* and means the binding back of man to God, there is no God in the system with whom man can be brought into such a connection. If religion comes from *relego* and means reverential communion with the Deity in true worship, there is no such

Being with whom man can be brought into such a fellowship. In all its effort to solve the problem of human existence and devise a way of deliverance from physical ills and moral evils, Buddhism ignores the idea of a God, and of man as a sinful being whose duty is to bring his moral nature into harmony with that God. Mohammedanism with Allah, Brahmanism with its pantheon of divinities, as well as Christianity with its eternal living Creator, are religions. They recognize some personal, supreme, divine Power to whom men have an unescapable relation of duty and service. Buddhism recognizes no divine way of salvation for man from his sinful state, which would naturally be his source of hope for deliverance from the thraldom of evil, but it leaves him to work out his own salvation, if it can be called a salvation.

Perhaps the broadest and most general Christian definition of religion is that of Schleiermacher, who says that it is a feeling of dependence. But in Buddhism there is no feeling of dependence save on self. " By one's self evil is done, by one's self we suffer; by one's self evil is left undone, by one's self one is purified. Purity and impurity belong to one's self, no one can purify another."[1]

Near the close of his life, Buddha, addressing Ananda, says: "Be yourselves your lamp, yourselves your refuge."[2] Without a God, without any supernatural revelation, without prayer, without real worship, without duties essentially religious, without a Saviour to make possible a pure, blissful, eternal deliverance from sin, Buddhism in itself must be refused the name of a religion. Yet it has been taken as a religion by vast numbers of mankind, and out of respect to this fact we must treat it as a religion when we consider its principles and doctrines.

Birthplace of Buddhism

BUDDHISM had its origin in that portion of the famous and fertile valley of the Ganges, still occupied by the ancient cities of Patna, Benares, and Oudh. A part of this territory belonged to Magadha, so celebrated in Buddhist annals, now known as Bihar, a corruption of Vihara Land, a

[1] *Dham.*, 165. [2] *Maha-pari-nibbana Sutta.*

name gained from the number of sacred buildings erected for the dwellings of monks, and for appointed Buddhist observances. It was here that Buddhism acquired its distinctive character before it spread to distant countries under the missionary zeal of the royal Asoka.

Environment of Gotama's Youth

AT the beginning of Gotama's career this region was under the sway of Brahmanism. It was formerly thought that Gotama's moving purpose was to be a great reformer, and Buddhism has been described as a strong reaction from, and a protest against Brahmanism as a whole. But investigation proves that there is no evidence that he ever intended to establish a new system in all respects radically opposed to Brahmanism. It is true that he rejected the supernatural revelation, sacerdotalism, priestly claims and minute ritual ceremonies of Brahmanism, but he adopted many of its doctrines and gave them an important position in his system. He never required his disciples publicly to renounce Brahmanism.

Though he always spoke against the priestly pretensions of the Brahmans and denied their idea of caste, he was kindly and temperate in his treatment of them, and even adopted the term Brāhmana as a designation of an Arhat, or one who has attained sanctification.[1] The Brahmans were the representatives of a supernatural revelation by whose authority they claimed sacerdotal powers. They alone could administer the complicated ritual which, with its sacrifices and tedious ceremonies, was essential to their mediatorship between men and gods. Gradually religion grew into a matter of mere ceremony without necessary connection with morality. The frequent lack of a moral life among the Brahmans and the arrogance of their priestcraft made the people grow weary of them and ready for some other system that would meet the needs of their human hearts. All these dogmas were rejected by Gotama.

But out of the religious environment in which he was brought up he accepted and incorporated into his system, with some modifications, many preexisting conceptions and principles. In the pantheism of

[1] Childers' *Dham.*, 383.

Brahmanism the great impersonal Brahm becomes conscious and personal in men. This severance of the soul of man from Brahm, the impersonal universe, is due to Ignorance and Illusion. When Ignorance and Illusion are dispelled by the knowledge that all personal existence is an unreality, the soul is reabsorbed in Brahm. Then all cause of suffering ends in his unconscious existence. With necessary modifications Gotama adopted Ignorance and Illusion as the ground of human existence. This gave the profoundly pessimistic character to his views of human life. Sickness, suffering, decay, and death are the inevitable attributes of existence. The refuge is to escape from existence into the unconscious calm of Nirvāna, at least a virtual extinction.

Brahmanism taught that, while a soul which had purified itself by good deeds and pierced the illusion of a separate existence would be absorbed in Brahm, those who had failed to do thus must pass through repeated rebirths until such purification and true knowledge had been attained. The basis of this doctrine of metempsychosis is the principle that punishment or reward must follow every act of a man, and that his present condition is the impartial and due result of the good or evil done in former existences. While rejecting the idea of a soul in man, Gotama adopted this principle in his doctrine of transmigration with all its gloomy prospect of numberless existences clouded with evil and suffering.

The Brahmanical doctrine of asceticism was a natural sequence. The world is evil, and renouncing the world is the safest mode of life. Gotama accepted this principle, although he rejected the self-inflicted penances and tortures to which Hindu ascetics looked as exceedingly meritorious and helpful.

It would then appear that Gotama, growing up in the environment of Brahmanism, shared the widespread dissatisfaction with much of that system of religion, but still approved of and adopted many of its important principles. He did not rise up as a violent antagonist of that faith, though he openly and unmistakably condemned what he considered false in doctrine or evil in practice. He stands forth more in the rôle of a quiet reformer whose relation to his ancestral faith gradually widened as time passed. Indeed, apparently no serious persecution of him or of his followers as they grew in number, ever took place. This exemption would not have been the case had his relation been that of an aggressive, hostile reformer.

In this historical origin of Buddhism there is something analogous to the origin of Christianity. Both religions grew out of systems extremely sacerdotal. Both discarded sacerdotalism, priestly claims, and a ceremonious ritual. Both retained certain great principles in the religions which they supplanted and made them vital parts of their doctrine. Both repudiated the narrowness that made the benefits of religion the privilege of a caste or race, and opened the ways of salvation (so different in themselves) to all men without distinction of birth or nationality.

We need to consider, not only the influence of the environment in the midst of which Gotama grew up, but an outline of his life, that we may form some conception of his personality which must have been an important factor in the development of his system. He elaborated his method by his own experience and thought, and from a story of his life we may gather some knowledge of the trend of his mind and the circumstances which favored the development of his ideas. Every founder of religion inevitably puts much of his personality into that religion. The personality of Christ is a vital element in Christianity. Such a religion as Buddhism must bear the impress of the mind and experience of its founder. Indeed, it is very much a revelation of its founder.

Sources of Information

But it is necessary first to inquire what are our sources of information. There is not space in this essay for an exhaustive critical discussion of the date of the formation of the Buddhist canon of the Hinayana school, as we now have it, which is accepted as authoritative by the Southern Buddhists. The three Pitakas undoubtedly were a gradual growth. They are not regarded as inspired like the sacred books of other religions. They are accepted as embodying the results wrought out by the natural processes of the thinking of Gotama's mind. So far as evidence goes, there is no indication that Gotama ever wrote down any of his precepts, much less any one of the books of the canon, although it is probable that writing was somewhat used in his time. He confined himself during the forty-five years of his itinerating ministry to the oral statement of his doctrine. It is difficult to say when and how the present books of the Pitakas were gathered in the three baskets or collections, the Sutta Pitaka, the Vinaya Pitaka, and the Abhidhamma Pitaka. The Buddhist statement is that the canon was settled at the First Council at Rajàgaha in the days immediately following the death of Gotama, and that it was afterward handed down by oral tradition; that about a hundred years later certain relaxations of the rules having arisen and caused divisions among the monks, a Second Council assembled at Vesali (or Vaisali) and the rules of the Sangha were again vindicated and confirmed; and that finally, owing to the rise of schismatic schools, a Third Council was convened by King Asoka at Pātaliputra (Patna) about 242 B. C., at which the canon was again solemnly rehearsed, considered, and confirmed in its present form. This statement cannot be accepted, as it involves much that is mythical. Oldenburg and Max Müller have exhaustive discussions of this subject. There is great doubt whether the First Council ever had an existence. Oldenburg thinks that it is a fictitious assembly. If it did assemble, it may have begun some arrangement of the teaching of Gotama, though it could have been nothing more than a local gathering of monks and does not deserve the name of a Sangiti. The Second Council was also apparently a purely local one, and its actual relation to the canon is uncertain. It is not until we come to Asoka's Council that we stand on clearly historical ground. It would seem that the Buddhist canon had a gradual development. Arguments to prove this may be drawn from the canon itself. From the fact that we have in the Pitakas no mention of the Third Council,[1] but have references to the First and Second Councils, the inference may be safely drawn that the canon was certainly closed at Pātaliputra 242 B. C. There are references to the first two Councils in the Cullavagga, showing that some portions of the present canon were of a later origin than others. The Cullavagga

1 Oldenburg's *"Vinaya Pitaka,"* Introd., p. 25.

declares that the presentation of doctrine at the First Council was along two lines, the Dhamma and the Vinaya, Ananda reciting the Dhamma, and Upali the Vinaya. The term Dhamma was doubtless used in a wide sense and included portions now placed in the Abhidhamma, of which there was no mention. The Patineokhha now included in the Vibhanga was certainly in existence at that time and was doubtless included in the Vinaya. This twofold division which must have been in existence before the Cullavagga, was a natural one—a collection of discourses on good and evil called Dhamma or Doctrine, and a collection of rules of discipline called Vinaya. As yet there was no need of the Abhidhamma or "further dhamma," which is supplementary to the Sutta Pitaka and also deals with metaphysical questions. The Abhidhamma could not have been added until after the Council of Vesali, for it is not referred to in the account of the proceedings of that body. The Abhidhamma was doubtless adopted at the time of the Third Council, and from that date the threefold division of the Pitakas has been accepted as the canonical scriptures of Buddhism. If this view is correct, there was a gradual development of the Buddhist scriptures from the time of Gotama to their final collection and arrangement in the reign of Asoka. Just how much of this mass of sacred writings which had been accumulating for two centuries is the actual teaching of Gotama himself cannot be ascertained, but there is little doubt that all the great fundamental doctrines, like the Four Noble Truths, the Nidāna, Nirvāna, etc., belong to him. However, for our purpose of examining Buddhism, it is necessary to take the canon as it is accepted by the Southern Buddhists.

In considering the life of Gotama we are at once met with the difficulty of knowing what is fact and what is legend. There is no distinct biography or memorabilia of Gotama analogous to what we find in the four Gospels. Personal disciples of Christ at no late date after his death gathered up the events of his life in sacred narratives that we possess. But evidently the life of the founder of Buddhism was an afterthought. Perhaps a reason for this was that the message of his disciples in their preaching was not only the doctrines but the person of Christ, whereas the disciples of

Gotama were concerned chiefly with his doctrine. The Gospels certainly emphasize the life of Christ much more than the Pitakas that of Gotama. It seems as if but little effort was at first made to picture the life of Buddha, and that it was only at a much later period that a detailed representation of his life was attempted. In the Pitakas we find minute details of the beginning of his ministry, especially in the first book of the Mahanagga, and of the close of his ministry in the Maha-parinibbana Sutta and in fragments scattered through the fifth book of the Mahanagga. There are also many references to him in connection with the utterance of discourses or the promulgation of rules, which may have a historical basis.

As the halo of tradition gathered around him, legends arose through the glowing imagination of fervent disciples, and myth and fable became attached to his name. Such are the birth stories of the five hundred and fifty Jātakas, many of which are modifications of ancient Indian folk-lore. They are doubtless the tribute of reverence from devout and zealous disciples for their teacher, and may not at first have been intended to be taken as a real history of

Gotama, but in time came to be so looked upon by men whose Oriental minds delight in what is graphic and marvelous, and are always inclined to give credence to such things, notwithstanding the exaggerations and puerilities involved. This legendary element is of no assistance in discovering the real events of Buddha's life. It is necessary to confine ourselves to the accounts of him found in the sacred books as accepted by the Southern Buddhists. Books of the Northern Buddhists, like the Lalita Vistara, do not concern us, as they belong to the Great Vehicle. The Maha-parinibbana in its present form may be of as late a date as the reign of Asoka, as Copleston thinks, but its internal character gives evidence that much of it is of an older date.

In the material that we have, there are salient events which cannot be relegated to myth, like the Enlightenment and the First Sermon, for they are necessary to the understanding of Buddhism itself. There are other events that fit so naturally into the place they occupy that they commend themselves as resting on a historical basis. By means of these events gathered out of a mass of legendary material, a substantially correct impression of Gotama and of his character may be gained. They seem to show a man of decided individuality of character, of personal attractiveness, having a profound knowledge of the workings of the human heart, kindly disposed towards his fellows, calm in spirit, loving contemplation, and imbued with a lofty moral ideal. So far as we can get a picture of his life, his character was one of the most lovely that has ever blessed the world.

Life of Gotama

GOTAMA was born at Kapila-vastu in Kosala (modern Oudh). The time of his birth is uncertain. The traditional date, about 542 B. C., is doubtless incorrect by at least nearly half a century. Probably the approximate date is about 500 B. C. The date of birth is determined from the date of his death at the age of eighty years. Various results have been arrived at by scholars. The date of his death has been placed by Max Müller at 477 B. C., by Oldenburg 430 B. C., by Williams 420 B. C., by Rhys Davids 412 B. C., and by Kern 370-380 B. C. The name given him as a child was Siddhārtha, one who has accomplished his purpose. Gotama appears to have been his family name. He doubtless assumed the title of Buddha at the time of his Enlightenment. All other names are titles applied to him by his disciples, as Sakẏamuni, the Sakya Sage, Jina the Conqueror, and many others.

His father was a Sakyan chief named Suddhadana. He was not a king in the modern sense of the term, but probably was the ruler of a large agricultural district occupied by his tribe. Whether the Sakyans were an Aryan tribe or came from Turanian stock beyond the Himalayas is uncertain. The Pitakas represent him as of the purest Kohatriya race on the side of both parents. If they were of the warrior caste their people seem to have been devoted to the cultivation of rice.

The incarnation of the Buddha is doubtless a myth of late date devised to enhance his glory. It bears a curious distant resemblance to the miraculous birth of Christ. The legend says that when the time came for him to be born as Buddha he assumed the form of a white elephant (which is regarded by Buddhists as an exceedingly precious and auspicious object), and descending from the Tushita heaven, entered the womb of his mother Maya, the elder of the two sisters, who were the wives of Suddhadana. When he was born, the god Brahma received him from the side of his mother, and after her death, seven days later, he was placed in the care of his aunt, Mahā-prajāpati, the younger wife.

As he grew up he seems to have been somewhat indisposed toward those manly, athletic exercises and vigorous contests that were customary for young men of the class to which he belonged. His relatives complained to his father about his remissness, as by this he would not be prepared to lead them successfully against their foes in time of war. In consequence of their complaint, Gotama fixed a day to display his attainments, and by his superior skill above all others in archery, and by his mastery in the "twelve arts" removed all distrust of his ability from the minds of his complainants.

He grew up surrounded by wealth and pleasure. Three palaces were provided for him, one for each of the three seasons, according to the Eastern idea of what was suitable for a prince.

There is no reason to doubt the main points of his marriage to Yasodharā, his cousin, and the birth of his son Rahula. This birth took place in the twenty-ninth year of Gotama's life. Evidently for a long time his attention had been dwelling on the ills and suffering existing in life. His keen eye had pierced the glittering covering of splendor and luxury that concealed so much evil and sorrow, and the suggestion of renouncing the world had been working in his mind. For when he learned the tidings that his wife had borne him a son, he saw that a new tie had come to bind him more strongly to his home and present life. If he was to enter the solitary life of a mendicant searcher after truth further delay would be dangerous, if not fatal, to his purpose.

The legend of the four visions, which purport to be the reason of his final decision, is picturesque and beautiful. It is probable that his frequent teaching of the impermanence of human existence and pleasure, shown by old age, disease, and death, led to the use of some such incident as the conversion of Yāsa, the sixth disciple to enter the Sangha, to give a foundation for the story in reference to Gotama, for Yāsa is represented as possessing three palaces and living in splendor, but having been roused from sleep one night, and having been disgusted at the appearance of his attendants who lay around him buried in sleep, he determined to abandon his luxurious life and become a follower of Buddha.

The Great Renunciation must certainly stand on a basis of fact. It is one of the three great central events of Gotama's life, according to the ideas of Buddhists. The idea of the innate evil in life, the illusory nature of all things, and the necessity of separation from the world, by which opportunity might be found to search for and achieve salvation, had been growing in Gotama's mind. With the birth of his son Rahula, when he was about thirty years old, evidently came the conviction that now he must take the great step of renouncing all, if the step was ever to be taken. It was a crisis in his career. Doubtless the declaration of the Khaggavisāna Sutta[1] is a correct reflection of his ideas, "He who has compassion on his friends and confidential (companions) loses (his own)

[1] *Sut. Nip.*, I., 3.

advantage, having a fettered mind; seeing this danger in friendship, let one wander alone like a rhinoceros." In his child he saw the strongest tie that would bind him to the world. There was no time to be lost. Beautiful with vivid coloring and quivering with natural human affection, the story tells of that long, last look at his wife and child, of his intense yearning to clasp his loved son once more in a paternal embrace, of the feverish haste with which he hurries forth to mount his favorite steed and fly far from home and friends, and of the studied attempts of Māra, the Evil Tempter, to turn him from his purpose by promises of splendid earthly rule and pleasures, and by appalling manifestations of physical terrors. But nothing deters the fugitive in his flight until he is beyond the reach of his father in another country. There he divests himself of his princely garments, cuts off his hair and goes forth a wandering mendicant. The bond joining him to the world is cut at last.

He has now the great object of search before him—salvation. As yet the way is not apparent. At Rājagaha he becomes the disciple of two Brahman philosophers, Alāra and Uddaka, who were doubtless teachers of some leading school of philosophy of that time. As their teaching did not satisfy his mind, he gave himself up to the extremest form of ascetic life by the practice of the most severe mortification of the body in the wood of Uruvelā, and reduced his food, as the story runs, till he ate only a single grain of rice a day. His self-imposed austerities were such as to awaken the astonishment of five hermits who had their abode near him. One day he fell to the ground and appeared to be dead. Recovering from his swoon, he became convinced that there was no way of salvation in philosophy or in physical austerities. He took food and, thereby having incurred the displeasure of his five fellow-hermits, removed to another place where he could have undisturbed solitude. Doubtless there is historical truth in this statement.

Now came a great epoch in his history. He was really taking the last steps toward the realization of the Great Enlightenment by which he attained Buddhahood. Seating himself under a banyan tree (*Ficus Religiosa*), he gave himself up to profound meditation. This tree henceforth became known as the sacred Bo Tree of the

Buddhists, from the root *budh* to know, as Gotama attained under it the full knowledge of the way of salvation. Absorbed in thought, he passed on through the stages of Thāna, but he was not left in quiet. Māra again assailed him with the memory of home, with the display of carnal pleasures, and with terrific visions of demons and hideous monsters. All was in vain. The mind of Gotama rose superior to all these temptations, and, ascending higher and higher, passed through the remaining four Samāpattis (of which the stages of Jhāna are the first four) until at last the illusions of Ignorance and Error passed away and the brilliant illumination of the Great Enlightenment, which he had so persistently and laboriously sought, filled his mind and satisfied his heart. He had attained Buddhahood. He was no longer a Bodhisatva, but a Buddha, an enlightened one. But this enlightenment was what? The gloomy conviction that all existence is suffering, that man must pass through numberless transmigrations until by a self-wrought virtue he could obtain deliverance, and passing into Nirvāna, extinguish existence.

The Buddhaship involved the proclamation of the enlightenment. From this he shrank. The Mahavagga[1] tells us that he was tempted to shirk the responsibility of preaching. Men were given to desire, intent on desire, and delighted in desire. If men were thus, they would not understand his doctrine, and his work would be a source of weariness and annoyance. These evil suggestions were attributed to Māra, and Mahabrahma is represented as, in the intensity of his desire for a favorable decision on the part of Buddha, descending and earnestly saying to Gotama, "Rise up, O Spotless One, and unclose the gates of Nirvāna. Rise up, and look upon the world lost in suffering. Rise up, go forth and proclaim the doctrine." Gotama yielded to the entreaty, and at the age of thirty-five began his ministry, which lasted until his death at eighty years of age.

While there are some superficial similarities to Christ's forty days of fasting in the wilderness and temptation by Satan, in the forty-nine days of Gotama's fasting and temptation by Mara, at the beginning of their respective ministries, vast is the difference of doctrine. The doctrine of the one

1 S. B. E., Vol. XIII., p. 84.

is bright with the heavenly light that enveloped the Holy Dove in his descent at the baptism, and is pervaded by the assurance of the divine testimony: "This is my beloved Son, in whom I am well pleased." [1] The doctrine of the other is dark with the world's woes and hopelessness, and has no divine voice giving confidence and the prospect of eternal deliverance and happiness.

Gotama starts forth on his mission. His first thought is to preach to his first two teachers, the Brahman philosophers, but they have already died. He then determined to find the five hermits who were neighbors so long in his secluded life at Uruvelā. Learning that they were in the Deer Park at Benares, he turned his steps thither. By the road he encountered Upaka, an ascetic, who inquired: "By the following of whose doctrine is the face of Gotama so radiant with happiness?" Gotama replied with joyful confidence: "I follow no teacher; I have overcome all foes and all stains; I am superior to all men and all gods; I am the absolute Buddha. And I am going now to Benares to set in motion the Wheel of the Law as a king the triumphant wheel of his

1 Matt. 3: 17.

kingdom. I am the Conqueror." Going forward, he met the five ascetics who, although they had agreed to treat him with only the barest civility, were soon converted to his doctrine, and with him formed the first Sangha of six members. To these five monks of the Sangha, Gotama delivered his first sermon, called the "Dhamma-cakkappavattana Sutta," the "discourse setting in revolution the Wheel of the Law."[1] In this discourse he sets forth the middle path which is the Noble Eightfold Path (*ariyo atthangiko Maggo*), and the Four Noble Truths (*ariya-saccani*), the consideration of which will be taken up later.

The winning of disciples very greatly prospered. Yasa, the son of a wealthy merchant, becomes the sixth disciple, and soon the number of monks increases to sixty. They belong to rich and prosperous families. These men, like the Seventy in the Gospels, are sent forth to proclaim the new doctrine. His commission is clear and explicit. They are commanded to go forth and wander everywhere, out of compassion to the world, that

[1] For discussion of Pali terms, see Rhys Davids' "Buddhism," p. 45, and "Childers' Dict.," p. 116.

they may benefit men by preaching the doctrine.

Gotama himself also went forth to do the same work. For at least eight months of the year he itinerated through the country, and when the rainy months (*was*) came, remained in retreat, in meditation and in giving instruction to his followers who gathered around him. There are only brief notices of personal events during his forty-five years' ministry until we come to the close of his life, which is narrated with much detail. On a hill—Gayāsīsa—he preached the famous fire-sermon, in which he declared that "Everything is burning" and compared all life to flame, giving numerous illustrations. It was early in his ministry that the great disciples Sāriputra, Moggellāna, Ananda, Upāli, and Kāsyapa attached themselves to him. Devadatta, who subsequently became his antagonist, also declared himself a disciple. After some personal opposition to the establishment of an order of female mendicants, he sanctioned the proposal and laid down rules for the guidance of such an order. In time an immense number of disciples gathered about him, according to the account, which is replete with exaggeration that the Oriental loves so much. The result was that his cousin and disciple Devadatta, moved by personal ambition, sought to persuade Gotama to make him the future leader of the disciples, as Gotama was advanced in years. Failing in this, Devadatta organized a schism and became the Judas of Buddhism.

The narrative of his visit to his father, and of the conversion of his son and other members of the family, is very touching and lifelike, and doubtless rests on a historical foundation.

When we come to the close of the ministry of Buddha the records become full and pictorial in statement. The Maha-parinibbana, "The Book of the Great Decease," details each stage of his last journey to Kusi-nagara, where he died, and his conversations with his loyal followers. As he felt his end approach he seemed to be anxious to improve every opportunity to enlighten and establish his followers in his doctrine. There is something intensely pathetic in the reiteration of doctrines that seem to us so pessimistic and gloomy, but seemed to him the only solution of the problem of existence. After Gotama's recovery from a serious illness near Vesali, Ananda, looking forward to Buddha's near death, begged him, ere his departure, to give final instructions about the Sangha. There is a tender tone of feeling verging on astonishment in the answer:

What then, Ananda, does the Order expect that of me? I have preached the truth without making any distinction between exoteric and esoteric doctrine; for, in respect of the truths, the Tathagata has no such thing as the closed fist of a teacher who keeps something back. Surely, should there be any one who harbors the thought, "It is I who will lead the Brotherhood," or "The Order is dependent on me," it is he who should lay down instructions in any matter concerning the Order. Now, the Tathagata harbors no such thoughts. Why, then, should he leave instructions in any manner concerning the Order? I too, O Ananda, am now grown old and full of years, my journey is drawing to a close. I have reached my sum of days. I am turning eighty years of age. And just as a worn-out cart can only with much additional care be made to move along, so methinks the body of the Tathagata can only be kept going with much additional care. . . Therefore, be ye lamps unto yourselves; be ye a refuge to yourselves. Betake yourselves to no external refuge. Hold fast to the truth as a lamp. Hold fast as a refuge to the truth; look not to any one for refuge besides yourselves.

After this Buddha is represented as having determined that after three months' time he would die, a resolve that, as the legend runs, could not be shaken by the temptations of Māra, and was marked by the occurrence of a tremendous earthquake. This decision was announced at a great assembly of the monks of Vesali in the Kūtāgāra Hall. He closed the discourse with the words:

> Behold now, monks, I impress it upon you; all (composite) things are subject to the law of dissolution; press on earnestly to perfection; soon the Tathagata's final extinction will take place; at the end of three months the Tathagata will enter on extinction.

He then left Vesali, and bidding the city a farewell by a long, parting look, went on his way from place to place, giving instructions as he went. When he arrived at Pāvā, a goldsmith by the name of Cunda prepared a meal of rice and pork. This was followed by violent dysentery. Disregarding this illness, he started for Kusi-nagara. Resting many hours by the river Kukushtā, half-way on his journey, he proceeded until he reached a grove outside of the city of Kusi-nagara. He was destined to go no farther. He knew that he was dying. Lying on a couch placed between two Sāl trees, he sent a message to Cunda to prevent regret at the result of his offering, comforted the grief-stricken Ananda with words of love and approval, entered into discussion with Subhadra, a Brahman, and converted him, proclaimed that after his death the Law would be in his place as teacher, and calling upon any one who was troubled with doubts to express them, that he might remove them and, having received no answer, declared that all present had entered into the path, beyond danger of return, which would lead to Nirvāna. Then after a little silence came the last words of the great teacher: "Behold, now, mendicants, I say to you, everything that exists must pass away; work out your own perfection with diligence."

The cremation of his body followed and was certainly attended with much pomp. This we conclude after allowance has been made for the extravagances which the growth of legend has interwoven with the narrative of the event.

This brief outline of the principal events in Gotama's life gives the picture of a man of high thought, lofty morality, and virtuous conduct. There was an intense honesty in his pursuit of truth, and fearlessness and patience in the promulgation of what he believed. But after granting all the beauty that appears in his life and character, that beauty falls short of the divine beauty of the life and character of the Perfect Man, in his sinlessness, in his lofty self-sacrifice, in his knowledge of God and man, in his apprehension of infinite truth, and in his full revelation of that truth to man. Gotama groped after truth, and when he attained what he considered the truth, it was a one-sided earthly system of philosophy. It was hopeless and depressing and had in it no good news. Christ knew truth, and when his revelation of it that embraced all conditions of man's nature, with all its needs, was finished, it was a gospel.

These great teachers were differently received. Gotama preached a doctrine of self-wrought righteousness, difficult in accomplishment, but pleasant to the pride of man. Christ preached a doctrine of righteousness that comes through the gracious assistance of God, in which works are of value as showing the presence of a divine life in the soul through faith, a doctrine always distasteful to the self-love of man. Consequently the narratives tell us that multitudes, the rich and powerful, became the disciples of Gotama, while only a few, generally the poor and humble, listened gladly to Christ. Both showed self-denial and self-abnegation, but in very different ways. One decrying human life and exalting the seclusion of a recluse, moved among men preaching a doctrine that, carried to its legitimate conclusion, was the enemy of all home and social life. The other, declaring human life a precious gift of God and exalting a life of busy helpfulness among men, preached a doctrine that was the promoter of a pure home and social life in the highest degree. The lives of Gotama and Christ were consistent with their teachings, but when we put the pictures side by side one is overshadowed with the gloom of a desired escape from existence; the other is radiant with the brightness of an expectation of a sinless, glorious, divine life. This seems to me an unescapable conclusion to the earnest and careful student as the portrait in the Pitakas is placed by the side of the portrait of the Evangelists.

The Ethics of Buddha

THE ethical teaching of Buddha is lofty and noble, and among the great religions of the world ranks next to that of Christianity. This teaching, designed for the production of virtuous character, is found not only in the Sutta Pitaka, but forms a large element in the Vinaya, and is scattered through Abhidhamma, which was long considered as only a depository of the metaphysics of Buddhism. A comprehensive view of this teaching as a harmonious whole can only be obtained by a comparison of different parts of the sacred books, as there is no connected treatment of the subject. But while there are many real as well as many superficial similarities to the moral teaching of Christianity, there are certain radically different fundamental principles underlying both systems of teaching which it will be necessary to examine after some of the similarities that exist have been pointed out. Some persons in Western lands have extolled the moral precepts of Buddhism, and compared them to the doctrine of the Sermon on the Mount. Others have exalted them even at the expense of Christianity, forgetting that over against all that is beautiful and true in them are to be placed the puerilities, the wearisome and useless repetitions,[1] the hair-splitting distinctions of terms, and the commands and prohibitions in the books of discipline whose translation could not find a place in any decent English publication. While facts do not, I think, bear out the views of such persons, it is just to accord the highest character to a large number of the Buddhist ethical precepts, as their intrinsic value demands.

The Buddhist ideal, for the attainment of which its ethical precepts are a guide, has the elements of gentleness, tranquillity, earnestness, and purity. The gentleness is an attitude of benevolent, kindly feeling toward all creatures. The tranquillity is a state of mind, calm, undisturbed by any congenial or uncongenial environment. The earnestness is a positive effort to be awake, vigilant, energetic, in an upright course of life that leads to the successful attainment of the highest and most perfect moral condition. Purity is the sinless moral state with no flaw of imperfection, passion, or feeling,

[1] Sir M. Williams quotes a most pertinent example from the Cullavagga in his "Buddhism," p. 541.

and is a necessary correlative of the tranquillity that is so important a part of the Buddhist ideal. Hence the moral tone of the Buddhist precepts is intensely earnest and has a real merit of its own. Their object was not simply an external morality, but an inward morality. Like Christianity, Buddhism in the application of these moral principles makes a distinction between those who follow the precepts outwardly and those who are actuated by a sincere inward desire to embody the precepts in their lives. As the evil springs from within, there can be no virtue which is not an inward overcoming of the evil. The Magha Sutta (862, 865) says: "Whence (do spring up) contentions and disputes, lamentation and sorrow, together with envy?" "From wish originate the (dear) objects of the world, and the covetousness that prevails in the world, and desire and fulfilment originate from it." Without inward sincerity as a possession, even a monk was one only in name. Yet all this high attainment in virtue, through the fulfilment of the precepts, did not have a correspondingly high aim to be reached by means of it. Its object was not the preparation for a sinless, pure, and immortal life in a blissful eternity, but was simply the destruction of the passions and desires that bind men to successive transmigrations and the dissipation of the ignorance which blind men's eyes to the fact that the true incidents of life are suffering and impermanence; and the cessation of all existence is the greatest of boons to be desired.

It must be remembered that while the moral precepts were deemed applicable to all Buddhists, yet only the members of the celibate Sangha, by following the special rules of monastic conduct together with the moral precepts, could possibly attain Nirvāna, the highest good. In view of the necessary conditions of life for those who could not enter the Sangha, Gotama established a secondary way for a laity, or "householders" (gahapati) as they were styled, who were to a certain degree associated with the Sangha as a recognized religious class of men. They might, through the observance of the precepts, attain a heavenly state (Sugati), but could never escape from the grip of Karma and existence. "The virtuous man is happy in this world, and he is happy in the next; he is happy in both. He is happy when he thinks of the good that he has done; he is still more happy when going on the good path."[1] Buddha, in reply to a question whether a virtuous householder who remained in the bond of married life could, after death, reach the end of sorrow, declared that it was impossible, but many such had reached a heavenly condition. To reach the end of sorrow the householder must enter the mendicant ranks, "Removing the characteristics of a gihin (householder) like a Pārikhatta tree whose leaves are cut off, clothed in a yellow robe after wandering away (from his house), let one wander alone like a rhinoceros."[2] The general precepts remain the same in application to the two classes, the Chikkhus and the Gahapatis, but the results are different in degree from the dissimilar condition of their modes of living.

Perhaps none of the rules for moral conduct are more prominent in the Buddhist system in the daily conversation of its followers than the five fundamental rules called the Panca sila:

1. One should not take life.
2. One should not steal.

[1] *Dham.*, 18. [2] *Khaggavisana Sutta*, 30.

3. One should not commit adultery.

4. One should not lie.

5. One should not drink intoxicating liquors.

These five commands are binding on all Buddhists, and are a part of Ten Precepts binding on all monks. Perhaps the five precepts were selected as of more universal application when the "householders" were recognized as an order by themselves. Once only in the Vinaya, the Five Precepts are quoted independently of the Ten Precepts for monks, in the story of the elephant, monkey, and partridge, who are said to have lived happily in the keeping of these precepts. In the same way they are mentioned in some of the Jātaka tales. They are stated with some diffuseness of wording in the Dhammika Sutta.[1]

"A householder's work I will also tell you, how a Savaka is to act to be a good one; for that complete Bhikkhu-dhamma cannot be carried out by one who is taken up by (worldly) occupations."

"Let him not kill, nor cause to be killed any living being, nor let him approve of others killing, after having refrained from hurting all creatures, both those that are strong and those that tremble in the world."

1 S. B. E., p. 65.

"Then let the Savaka abstain from (taking) anything in any place that has not been given (to him) knowing (it to belong to another) let him not cause any one to take, nor approve of those that take, let him avoid all (sort of) theft."

"Let the wise man avoid an unchaste life as a burning heap of coals; not being able to live a life of chastity, let him not transgress with another man's wife."

"Let no one speak falsely to another in the hall of justice or in the hall of the assembly, let him not cause (any one) to speak (falsely) nor approve of those that speak (falsely); let him avoid all (sort of) untruth."

"Let the householder who approves of this Dhamma, not give himself to intoxicatin drinks; let him not cause others to drink, nor approve of those that drink, knowing it to end in madness."

The five additional precepts for a monk, concern external practice and have no particular moral element in them save the cultivation of humility and soberness of life.

It may be well to consider here the third of the Five Precepts a little more closely. Entire abstinence from sexual intercourse was obligatory upon the monk. Without this abstinence one could not enter upon the direct path to Arhatship and Nirvāna. A wise man should avoid married life as if it were "a burning pit of live coals." In the

Muni Sutta (206) it is said: "From acquaintanceship rises fear, from household life arises defilement; the houseless state, freedom from acquaintanceship, this is indeed the view of a Muni." So intent was Buddha's purpose to cause the carrying out of this perfect chastity by monks that the Pātimokkha, which is a kind of manual to aid monks in clearing themselves from guilt by confession and is elaborated on the basis of the first four of the Five Precepts (violations of which are irremediable faults or "conditions of defeat"), has a large number of questions in regard to sexual intercourse too vile to be translated, and illustrations by pretended cases, which can only tend to pollute the minds of the monks by evil suggestions.[1]

In all this doctrine that the idea of marriage or a happy home life is evil, there was a direct antagonism to human nature. Such means as are employed in the Pātimokkha defeat themselves, for they cannot fail of producing unsavory moral results in the minds and practice of many of the monks. The doctrine is also in direct antagonism to

[1] See Copelston's article, July, 1888, "Contemporary Review."

the biblical teaching, that it is not good for man to be alone, which Christ approved by his teaching in regard to marriage, and by his presence at the feast of Cana. Naturally there came a recoil from the universal application of this doctrine of celibacy.

Apparently the doctrine was at first received without opposition. But as Gotama became successful in winning large numbers of disciples, the people complained, "Gotama is breaking up family life. He is leading away all Sanj'aya's followers. Whom will he take next?" They saw that the perpetuation of the race must give place to childlessness and the extinction of the family. It was necessary to have a relaxation of the rule. Marriage must be allowed, and so the "householder" was allowed to enter that state, and its upright, moral character in his case was assured by the approval of Gotama. It is placed among the blessed states described in the Mangala Sutta. In this Sutta the married man is exhorted to perform his family duties faithfully. It is a curious case of indulgence to a form of desire; desire being regarded by Gotama as one of the great evils of human nature. Granting the truth of his doctrine of celibacy as an essential condition to the highest excellence, what is the morality of such an indulgence? One cannot help feeling that there is a great contrast between the high moral basis on which the Christian doctrine of marriage rests, and the contradictory basis, according to Gotama's fundamental principle of celibacy, on which the "householder's" marriage rests.

The moral tone of the Mangala Sutta, which is a Sutta for laymen, is excellent. Allusion has already been made to the duties of a married man to his family. A few quotations will show their character:

> Waiting on mother and father, protecting child and wife, and a quiet calling, this is the highest blessing.
>
> The bestowing of alms (on monks), a righteous life, help given to relations, blameless deeds, these are the greatest blessing.
>
> Reverence and a lowly mind, contentment and gratitude, listening to the Law on proper occasions, these are the greatest blessing.

There are many precepts directed against the evil of the vices inherent in human nature.

In regard to Anger, the Dhammapada says:

"He who holds back rising anger like a rolling chariot, him I call a real driver; other people are but holding the reins" (222).

"Beware of bodily anger, and control thy body!" (231.)

"Beware of the anger of the tongue, and control thy tongue! Leave the sins of the tongue, and practise virtue with thy tongue" (232).

"Beware of the anger of the mind, and control thy mind! Leave the sins of the mind, and practise virtue with thy mind" (233).

"Him I call indeed a Brahmana who is tolerant with the intolerant, mild with faultfinders, and free from passion among the passionate. Him I call indeed a Brahmana from whom anger and hatred, pride and envy have dropped like a mustard seed from the point of a needle" (406-7).

Hatred: "For hatred does not cease by hatred at any time; hatred ceases by love, this is an old rule" (*Dham.* 5).

Pride: "Let him (the bhikkhu) learn every Dhamma inwardly or outwardly: let him not therefore be proud, for that is not called bliss by the good. Let him not therefore think himself better (than others or) low or equal (to others); questioned by different people, let him not adorn himself" (*Suvataka Sutta* 917, 918; *Sut. Nip.* IV., 14).

The person who, without being asked, praises his own virtue and (holy) works to others, him the good call ignoble, one who praises himself" (*Dutthatthaka Sutta*, 782; *Sut. Nip.*, IV., 3).

Hypocrisy: "Many men whose shoulders are covered with the yellow gown are ill-conditioned and unrestrained; such evil-doers by their evil deeds go to hell" (*Dham.*, 307).

"What is the use of platted hair, O fool! What of the raiment of goatskins? Within thee there is ravening, but the outside thou makest clean" (*Dham.*, 394).

Love of Evil Company: "He who walks in the company of fools suffers a long way: company with fools, as with an enemy, is always painful; company with the wise is pleasure, like meeting with kinsfolk" (207).

Love of riches: "These *sous* belong to me, and this wealth belongs to me, with such, a fool is tormented. He himself does not belong to himself; how much less *sous* and wealth?" (*Dham.*, 62.)

"What shall I eat, or where shall I eat?—he lay indeed uncomfortably (last night)—where shall I lie this night? Let the Sekha, who wanders about houseless, subdue these lamentable doubts. Having had in (due) time both food and clothes, let him know moderation in this world for the sake of happiness; guarded in these (things) and wandering restrained in the village let him, even (if he be) irritated, not speak harsh words" (*Sariputta Sutta* 970-71; *Sut. Nip.*, IV., 16).

Precepts in regard to other vices might be quoted were there space. The Ten Fetters (Samyojanas) as evil states of mind enter into the Buddhist system of morals, but they will be considered elsewhere.

The Ten Perfections (Pārimitas) are an unscientifically arranged set of transcendent virtues, the perfect exercise of which belong only to those who are in the path of Arhatship, and are a condition of the attainment of Nirvana. But underlying them are virtuous principles which are recognized and inculcated as desirable by all.

Love or Loving-kindness (mettain) is very fully dwelt on:

"Let us live happily then, not hating those who hate us! Among men who hate us let us dwell free from hatred" (*Dham.*, 197).

"And let him cultivate good-will towards all the world, a boundless (friendly) mind, above and below and across, unobstructed, without hatred, without enmity" (*Metta Sutta*, 149; *Sut. Nip.*, I., 8).

This is an attitude of kindly, compassionate feeling and not necessarily a motive of action. It seeks concord with others. "Do not speak harshly to anybody, those who are spoken to will answer thee in the same way" (*Dham.*, 133). "He abused me, he beat me, he defeated me, he robbed me—in those who do not harbor such thoughts hatred will cease" (*Dham.*, 4). It also abstains from doing injury to others: "Whosoever in this world harms living beings, whether once or twice born, and in whom there is no compassion for living beings, let one know him as an outcast" (*Vasala Sutta*, 116; *Sut. Nip.*, I., 7).

Self-control is a law of life. "As rain does not break through a well-thatched house, passion will not break through a well-reflecting mind." "If one man conquer in battle a thousand times thousand men, and if another conquer himself, he is the greatest of conquerors" (*Dham.*, 13, 103).

Forbearance: "Silently shall I endure abuse as the elephant in battle endures the arrow sent from the bow, for the world is ill-natured." "No one should attack a Brahmana, but no Brahmana (if attacked) should let himself fly at his aggressor! Woe to him who strikes a Brahmana, more woe to him who flies at his aggressor!" (*Dham.*, 320, 389.)

Recognition of Equality: "I do not call a man a Brahmana because of his origin or of his mother. He is indeed arrogant and he is wealthy; but the poor, who is free from all attachments, him I call indeed a Brahmana" (*Dham.*, 396).

Filial Love: "The gift of the whole world with all its wealth would be no adequate return to parents for all that they have done" (*Augut.*, II., 4).

Reverence for Age: "He who always greets and constantly reveres the aged, four things will increase to him, viz.: Life, beauty, happiness, power" (*Dham.*, 109).

"Let him dutifully maintain his parents, and practise an honorable trade; the householder who observes this strenuously goes to the gods by name Sayampabhas" (*Dhammika Sutta* 403; *Sut. Nip.*, II., 14).

Liberality is enforced, but it is not necessarily generous giving to others. It has a special Buddhist sense. Danam is a term meaning giving to the monks. This giving is simply for the purpose of reaping the personal benefit of the " merit " that follows as a reward. Unlike the Christian idea of giving, it is restricted in its exercise to almsgiving to a class of religious mendicants. It lacks the noble, uplifting, unselfish motive of generous kindness to others as a true service of God, the Supremely Perfect Being. The reward of giving comes to the Christian, but that reward is not the object of his giving, as merit is the object of the " liberality " of the Buddhist.

It is impossible in this essay to go into further detail in regard to the various phases of the Buddhist ethical system. It is a beautiful and noble system, showing a high ideal of personal kindness, moral earnestness, and purity. But when we look at the basis on which the system is reared, and compare it with that on which the Christian system of ethics rests, there are profound and radical differences that appear at once. The moving spirit of Buddhist morality is selfish. It is a self-repression for the express benefit of self, and that benefit, when it culminates, is the extinction of all consciousness of self in Nirvāna. It starts with the assumption that all existence is suffering and is impermanent in character, and it uses its noble moral principles as a means by which the personal individuality of a man may be finally destroyed.

The moving spirit of Christianity is unselfishness. Its self-sacrifice is for the good of others as a service of God. Morality is what makes that unselfishness genuine and lofty in character. The object is not the direct benefit of self, but the pleasing of God, and the benefits which accrue to its possessor are attendant results and not the motives of moral action. Life is looked upon as a holy gift of God which is to stretch on through endless ages. Self-repression is exercised only so far as it is necessary to have the soul's moral feelings and condition harmonize with the perfect character of God and insure a sinless, blissful life in the endless hereafter. The sense of duty and the appeals of conscience are lacking as motives in Buddhist morality. The lack of the deep sense of obligation that arises from these as motives puts the earnestness inculcated by it on a low and purely selfish plane.

A man seeks to embody the moral teachings in order to attain the highest reward of Buddhism, only as it pleases himself. There is no obligation to any being or thing outside of himself. The emotions also must be repressed as variant forms of desire (tanhā). Love, kindness, pity, are rather passive tempers of the mind than active feelings. All forms of desire are looked upon as tending to evil, and an emotionless state is pictured as a desirable and glorious attainment. In Christianity the feelings are recognized as legitimate forces, to which appeal may be made in seeking advancement in moral good. Right desires, holy love, righteous anger, a reasonable fear, have their place as motives in Christian ethics.

If the comparison made here is correct, the superiority of the Christian ethical system is evident. Its foundation is the service of God. The motives that urge that service are pure and unselfish and contemplate the attainment of the highest form of life possible—a perfect, everlasting life in harmonious sympathy with the life of God. On the other hand, the Buddhist ethical system, looking upon life as intrinsically evil, has its foundation in the service of self. The motives that urge its practice in life are purely selfish and in the spirit of bald pessimism contemplate the final extinction of existence as the goal to be striven for. Such, I believe, is the great and unreconcilable difference that lies at the basis of the two systems.

Doctrine of God

HAVING, so far as space would allow, considered the ethical system of Buddhism, it is well to examine in connection with it certain great doctrines that in some form find their place in every religion, beginning with the doctrine of God.

The system of Buddha is unquestionably atheistic. He makes no recognition of a personal Supreme Being. In a conversation between him and Alāra, the wisest of the Brahmans, concerning the existence of an Isvara or Supreme God, Alāra declares the Great Brahma to be such a God. But Gotama objected that at the destruction of this universe at the end of a kalpa, such a Being could not exist; and that, had all things been created by such a Being, there could have been no possibility of evil and suffering, for all things must have been good. Declining further discussion as a profitless inquiry, he characterized himself in having taken part in it as one "who participates in the great mass of evil which exists and who seeks only a physician."[1]

Yet the need of some object of reverence and worship made itself felt. The natural tendency to require external aid in which one could put his trust, led to the elevation of Gotama into a sort of deification as an object of adoration, and his images have been set up in uncounted numbers in every country that has received any form of Buddhism. Divine attributes of infinite power and omniscience have been attributed to him. He is excellent above all other things. He "is the joy of the whole world; the helper of the helpless; the déva of dévas; the Brahma of Brahmas; the very compassionate; more powerful than the most powerful; able to bestow Nirvāna on him who only softly pronounces his name or gives in his name a few grains of rice. The eye cannot see anything, the ear cannot hear anything, nor the mind think anything

[1] Hardy's Manual, p. 375.

more excellent or more worthy of regard than Buddha."[1]

This semi-deification also showed itself in accepting the Buddha's teaching as infallible, and worshiping his Law as an embodiment of him after his entrance into Pari-nirvana. Whether intentionally or not, Buddha gave his influence to this end and made his direct teaching trend in that direction. When he found himself about to die he called Ananda and said: "It may be, Ananda, that in some of you this thought may arise: The words of our teacher are ended; we have lost our master. But it is not thus. The truths and rules of the Order which I have taught and preached, let these be your teacher when I am gone."[2]

The Sangha, or Community, the entire monastic fraternity, comprising all monks on earth and the saints in any other part of the universe who have not yet reached perfection, came to be looked upon as a collective unity or personification of the body of true disciples, and were accorded a place in the reverence of Buddhists. In this way the Buddhist Triad, Buddha, the Law, and

[1] Hardy's Manual p. 360.
[2] *Maha-parinibbana Sutta,* VI., 1.

the Sangha became objects of adoration, and in the absence of a Supreme God were made to occupy his place. These are the three refuges in which the Buddhist places his trust and are expressed in the universally used formula:

Buddham saranam gacchami.
Dhammam saranam gacchami.
Sangham saranam gacchami.

It is also an outcome of the atheistic character of Buddhism that Brahma and Indra were dethroned from the supreme seats that they occupied in Brahmanism, and with a host of deities (devas) placed in a position inferior to Buddha. For instance, Brahma begs Buddha to have compassion on men, and preach his doctrine. He pays religious honors to a robe that had been thrown aside by Buddha. The relations of Indra to Gotama always involve the acknowledgment of Gotama's superiority. The Buddha, the Enlightened Man, is the most superlatively excellent being among all beings of this or other worlds.

As might be expected from what has been said, there is no place for prayer in Buddhism. There is no God to whom the aspirations of the human soul may go forth, and whose divine assistance may be craved. The operation of natural laws is inexorable and is presided over by no Supreme Being. Therefore prayer, however sincere and earnest, is useless. Yet men in their sense of weakness and need crave some form of supplication. Hence prayer-formulæ, which are rather the expression of wishes than proper prayers, have been composed and are heard at every Buddhist shrine. They are thought to be in some way efficacious in bringing about the fulfilment of the desires of the offerer. There is no person to answer them, but they are supposed to come under some subtle, unknown law that is effective in its operation. These efficacious wishes are of four kinds: (1) the assignment of one's own merit to some one else; (2) the application to one's self or to others of the merits of Buddha; (3) the direction of the merit of a particular meritorious action of one's self to a special desired object (*Patthana*), and (4) the Act of Truth (*Saccakiriya*). Many times I have asked worshipers on the platform of the great Shwe Dagôn Pagoda at Rangoon and elsewhere, "Are you praying to Gotama or to the Pagoda?" The answer has always been,

"I am praying to no one." "For what are you praying, then?" "Nothing," is the inevitable reply. "I hope in some way, I know not how, to get benefit."

With no God, no divine Helper, with no one into whose ears prayer can enter, and from whom aid and blessing can come, there are a darkness and hopelessness in Buddhism that are only intensified by contrasting these facts with the fact of the existence of the Eternal God, the loving Father of Christianity, whose ears are ever open to hear the cry of his children and whose succor ever comes to them in their need, bringing with it brightness and living hope into their lives.

The World

THE sublime sentence that opens the book of Genesis, "In the beginning God created the heavens and the earth," has no counterpart in the Pitaka. As there is no idea of a Supreme God in the Buddhist scriptures, so there is no idea of an Omnipótent Creator, either bringing matter into existence by his own will or developing phenomena from some eternally existent substance. As in the question of the existence of a God, so in the question of the primary origin of things, Gotama regarded any attempt to solve it as without benefit. He was content to leave the mystery an unsolved problem. Sir Monier Williams puts the matter very concisely: "Buddhism has no Creator, creation, no original germ of all things, no soul of the world, no personal, no impersonal, no supramundane, no ante-mundane principle."[1]

At the same time Gotama refused to discuss the eternity of the existing universe. "When Mālunka asked Buddha whether the existence of the world is eternal or not eternal, he made no reply; but the reason of this was, that it was considered by the teacher as an inquiry that tended to no profit."[2] His method is well illustrated in some questions addressed to him in Vacchagotta's Fire Sutta:[3] "Do you hold the view that the world is eternal?" He answered: "No." "That the world is not eternal?" "No." "That it has an end?" "No." "That is has not an end?" "No."

Yet Buddhism has its cosmology, for as

[1] "Buddhism," p. 117. [2] Hardy's Manual, p. 375.
[3] *Maj. Nih.*, 72.

Rhys Davids says, "Buddhism takes as its ultimate fact the existence of the material world and of conscious beings living within it." But this universe came from nothing and will resolve itself into nothing. There have been previous universes, each with its revolution of myriad cycles of years, followed by a great cataclysm of destruction. This universe, with its central mountain Meru and its strange concentric seas, its ten thousand worlds with their attendant heavens, earth of continents, hells and ruling deities, after the passage of immense cycles of time, a conception of which the mind fails to grasp, will come to its complete dissolution, to be succeeded by a new universe, made, not from the material of its ruins which has altogether ceased to be, but rising from nothing as a completely new universe. The cause of the new universe is Karma, the potent energy accumulated in the existence of the preceding universe which brings another into existence after that has disappeared forever. Sir Monier Williams calls it "act-force." This Karma acts in the same way as in all sentient beings. Childers quotes a passage in the Dictionary which shows this: "*Kam-*

manā vattati loke kammana vattati pajā," "Through Karma the world of sentient beings exists, from Karma all creations derive their existence."

The Christian system is the opposite of the Buddhist system at almost every point. Its Supreme Being, the Creator, presides over a universe which he has brought into existence, and which, when its time of probation is finished, will be transformed into a new heavens and earth, in which freedom from sin and active holiness will reign without a disturbing element.

The Doctrine of Man

THE teaching of Buddhism in regard to man is quite consistent with its doctrine of the world. As there is no Divine Self, no Presiding Spirit in the universe, so there is no soul (ātman) in man. In Buddhism it is his terrible Ignorance (Avijja) that makes a man think "I am." Such belief is regarded as one of the worst forms of heresy. It occupies the first place in Three Great Delusions, and is called Sakkāyaditthi. It is also called Attavāda, "the doctrine of the existence of a soul," and finds its place among the four Upādānas which are the cause of birth and all the evils of existence resulting from it.

In the Questions of Milinda (Menander) occurs the oft-quoted dialogue between King Milinda and the Sage Nāgasena, in which the existence of a personal Ego is denied. When asked his name, Nāgasena replied: "I am called Nāgasena by my parents, priests, and others. But Nāgasena is not a separate entity." The king is puzzled, feeling that there can be no virtue nor vice, no reward nor punishment. Naming the parts of the body, the mind and the Skandhas, he asks concerning each one, whether it is Nāgasena. When the Sage replied "No," the king replied: "Then I do not see Nāgasena. Nāgasena is a sound without meaning. You have spoken untruth. There is no Nāgasena." Taking a chariot as an illustration, the sage shows that only when the different parts are united or combined is there a chariot. In like manner, "as the various parts of a chariot form, when united, the chariot, so the five Skandhas, when united in one body, form a being, a living existence. Rhys Davids naïvely comments on this conclusion: "Whatever we may think of the argument, it is at least clear that a soul is just as much and just as little acknowledged in man as a separate *substance* is acknowledged in a chariot."

Instead of a permanent, individual, immortal soul as Christianity declares, or a soul existing in the body and migrating from one body to another as Brahmanism teaches, Gotama declared that all sentient beings were a combination or assemblage of certain constituent elements or faculties, which is not a soul or self. These elements which are called Skandhas, do not exist after death, but disappear with the dissolution of the body. As the body constantly changes by death, so do the Skandhas constantly change. They combine at each birth, dissolve at each death, and fresh Skandhas combine at each rebirth. The Skandhas are: (1) Rupa, form (of which there are twenty-eight properties). (2) Vedanā, sensation (having six classes, according as they arise from the contact of the five senses and the mind with external objects, each class also having a further triple division as it may be either pleasant, unpleasant, or indifferent). (3) Sanna, perception (Rhys Davids, Abstract Ideas), springing from the six kinds of sensation. (4) Sankhāra, Aggregations (Rhys Davids, Tendencies or Potentialities), *i. e.* mental properties or tendencies of sentient being, of which there are fifty-two. (5) Vinnana, the thought faculty, combining consciousness and thinking, of which there are eighty-nine subdivisions. This is nearest to the idea of soul of anything that exists in the Pitakas, but like the other Skandhas, it ceases to be when the body dies.

But though the Skandhas disappear on the dissolution of the body, by means of the action of Karma, a new set of Skandhas comes into existence in a new being. Theoretically, there is no continuity of personal identity, for there is no soul. Only a man's Karma remains, and this necessitates the birth of a being in the world of men, beasts, or dévas, or in one of the hells. There is no consciousness of identity with the former being, nor will the former being experience any consciousness of reward or of retribution in the new birth.[1]

[1] This, however, is not so regarded by the uneducated common people of Burma, who fear the future,

In Christianity there is a soul. This soul is a divine creation, akin to the Spirit of God, immortal, priceless in value, ever maintaining its conscious identity throughout its endless existence. The idea of man is ennobled by the possession of a soul, as it is equally degraded when it is deprived of what really gives personality and individuality.

The Buddhist view of the body is, that it is a mass of corruption, to be looked upon with loathing, the abode of evil, the prison-house of man. "Look at this dressed-up lump, covered with wounds, joined together, sickly, full of many thoughts, which has no strength, no hold! This body is wasted, full of sickness, and frail, this heap of corruption breaks to pieces, life indeed ends in death."[1] The novice, when invested with the yellow robe, recites the verses which enumerate the thirty-two impurities of the body. The worthlessness of the body is detailed with a sickening minuteness in the Vijaya Sutta,[2]

seeming to think that they themselves will be reborn. I have even met here and there a man among the Buddhist Shans, who honestly professed to remember something of his preceding existence. I could never discover the source of the impressions of mind that gave rise to the idea in such a person.

[1] *Dham.*, 147, 148. [2] *Sut. Nip.*, I., 11.

which is too long to quote here. The body is considered a hindrance to advance in the path of sanctification, and must be repressed. "After a stronghold has been made of the bones, it is covered with flesh and blood, and there dwell in it old age and death, pride and deceit."[1] In the Sūciloma Sutta,[2] Buddha says: "Passion and hatred have their origin from this (body); disgust, delight, and horror arise from this body; arising from this (body) doubts vex the mind, as boys vex a crow." The action of each sense is to be watched, to be crushed as far as possible. There must be a constant guard lest any pleasure or pain, arising from the exercise of the bodily senses, finds a home in his consciousness and nourishes desire.

It is this character attributed to the body and the exercise of the senses that underlies the establishment of a monastic community in the Sangha. An ascetic life, a separation from the world, is the only method by which there can be a quick and sure advance in a virtuous life. All contact with the world only creates the excitement of earthly desires. A lonely, solitary life by

[1] *Dham.*, 150. [2] *Sut. Nip.*, III., 12.

which one's attention and thought will not be diverted from that meditation and conquest of self so essential to advancement towards the highest spiritual attainments, is deemed an absolute necessity. It is the discipline by which the glorious state of Nirvāna can be reached. "A wise man should leave the dark state (of ordinary life) and follow the bright state (of the Bhikkhu). After going from his home to a homeless state, he should in his retirement look for enjoyment where there seemed to be no enjoyment. Leaving all pleasures behind, and calling nothing his own, the wise man should purge himself from all the troubles of the mind."[1] "But they whose whole watchfulness is always directed to their body, who do not follow what ought not to be done, and who steadfastly do what ought to be done, the desires of such watchful and wise people will come to an end."[2] The Bhikshuvagga in the Dhammapada (360-382) gives a vivid delineation of the intense effort that should be made by a monk in the secluded life of self-repression prescribed for him. The Dhammika Sutta also contains a simi-

[1] *Dham.*, 87, 88. [2] *Dham.*, 293.

lar presentation of the subject. Hence, in addition to moral rules naturally arose various rules of discipline instituted for the guidance of the Sangha. The Four Resources lay at the basis of the external, ceremonial part of monastic life. These were the minimum of what was necessary in dwelling, dress, food, and condiments. So important were these deemed that the Vinaya enters with minute details concerning them. Rules were also laid down for the admission of members, for the gathering of monks on the reposatha or fast days, for confession and for *was* or retreats in the rainy season, about the months of June to August. Only a few rules were given for the regulation of the daily occupation of a monk's time, but the monk was left much freedom to spend the hours of his solitary life as seemed best to himself.

The ascetic life does not belong to true Christianity. By it the man is put into family and social relations. The body is looked upon as a wonderful creation, to be kept with care and made fit to be the dwelling-place of the Spirit of God. It is not evil in itself, and the right use of its powers and faculties in the service of God is emphatically enjoined. Christianity commands men not only to present their bodies as living sacrifices, holy, acceptable to God, in this life, but to expect hereafter a raised body, glorious in its perfection, the pure, everlasting home of a pure and holy spirit.

Character of Man's Present Existence

GOTAMA'S view of human life as evil was not an original doctrine with him. It was an almost universal one in India in his era, and was one of the principal features of Brahmanism. The ills and calamities of this present existence pressed on the spirits of men with a gloom that largely shut out a real appreciation of its blessings, and cast its shadow over all possible future existences, so that absorption in Brahm or disappearance in Nirvāna was the illusory light that illuminated the future. The result was that the truly religious man's life became, not a search for happiness, but a flight from evil. Then if the representation that runs through the account of Gotama's personal history can be trusted, the life that belonged to him as a prince and was deemed most valuable and desirable by his parents and companions, repelled his thoughtful mind as having only a false, transient brightness that covered an appalling inherent state of evil. As the result of his observation and profound thought, he made suffering a principal characteristic of existence. With no God in his system he could not rise to the Christian conception of suffering, as the result of sin through transgression, and by God's help a means of purifying and perfecting human character.

In his first sermon in the Deer Park at Benares, called "Dhammacakkappavattana Sutta," "the discourse that set rolling the wheel of the law," he laid down his doctrine in the Four Noble Truths. This doctrine is found in the Mahavagga, and was delivered to the five ascetics who, with himself, formed the first Sangha. It gives the fundamental principles of his system. He prefaces his statement of them by showing that men ought to pursue a Middle Path, avoiding both the extreme of a life which gives rein to the indulgence of the pleasures of sense which are degrading, vulgar, sensual, ignoble, useless, and the extreme of a life in which self-mortification is practised which is also painful, base, and profitless. This Middle Path was eightfold in nature and was the only true way by which one could advance in a virtuous life. It consisted of: (1) Right belief or views. (2) Right feelings or aim. (3) Right speech. (4) Right action. (5) Right livelihood. (6) Right endeavor or training. (7) Right memory or mindfulness. (8) Right meditation in concentration of the mind.

Having laid down these rules, Gotama proceeded to state that the reason for the establishment of the Middle Path arose from the Four Noble Truths: (1) Suffering—the fact that existence in this or any other world inevitably involves pain and sorrow. (2) The Cause of Suffering—the fact that lust (rāgā) or desire (tanhā) is seen in the thirst or craving for sensual pleasures, for worldly prosperity and for existence. (3) The Cessation of Suffering—the fact that suffering disappears with the conquest and extinction of lust and desire. (4) The Path leading to the Cessation of Suffering—the fact that perseverance in this path produces a virtuous life whose consummation is the destruction of all the causes of suffering. "There is no suffering for him who has finished his journey, and abandoned grief, who has freed himself on all sides, and thrown off all fetters." [1]

Suffering as the principle of all life is thus explained: "Birth is suffering; decay is suffering; sickness is suffering; death is suffering; association with things that we hate is suffering; separating from things that we love is suffering; failure to get what we crave is suffering; clinging to the five constituent parts of existence is suffering; perfect cessation of thirst and desire is the cessation of suffering. This is the Noble Truth of Suffering." There is here even a more dreary, desert-like view of life, more absolutely depressing and hopeless than that presented in the gloomy experience of the book of Ecclesiastes.

The pessimism of the Buddhist apprehension of the character of life has had advocates in all ages. In modern times the dismal pages of Schopenhauer and Von Hartman furnish an example of this mode of thinking. Gotama made Ignorance (avijjā) the first cause of the suffering and sorrow of existence, and placed it at the head of the twelve-linked Chain of Causalitv (Patic-

[1] *Dham.*, 90.

ca samuppada). This ignorance was the not knowing that all life is suffering, and that this suffering is the result of indulging in lusts and desires, and will cease only when lusts and desires are completely conquered and destroyed. The line of reasoning in the Chain of Causality is not very logical. Oldenburg, with all his mental acumen, says: "It is utterly impossible to trace from the beginning to end a connected meaning in this formula." From Ignorance arises sankhāra, a union of mental tendencies, the result of previous birth, which form character (also placed among the Skandhas); from this union of mental tendencies arises vinnāna, consciousness; from consciousness arises nāma-rūpa, individual being (name and corporeal form); from individual being arises salāyatana, the six organs of sense (*i. e.*, including the mind); from the six organs of sense arises phassa, contact; from contact arises vedanā, sensation; from sensation arises tanhā, desire; from desire arises upādāna, clinging (to existence); from clinging to (existence) arises chava, continuity of existence; from continuity of existence arises jati, birth; from birth arise jaramarana, old age and death, sorrow, lamentation, pain, grief, and despair. In this Paticca samuppāda we have the sequences starting with Ignorance, of the Four Noble Truths as the primal cause, and ending in suffering as the resultant characteristic of all conscious life.

One particularly evil form of Ignorance was the forgetfulness of the great fact that impermanence and change are inherent elements of existence. "He who knows that his body is like froth and has learnt that it is as unsubstantial as a mirage, will break the flower-pointed arrow of Māra, and never see the king of death." "All created things perish; he who knows and sees this becomes passive in pain; this is the way to purity."[1] "For there is not any means by which those that have been born can avoid dying; after reaching old age there is death; of such a nature are living beings."[2] The upadana, clinging to existence, in its four constituent parts, was most earnestly and pointedly denounced. It was an illusion so universally and persistently cherished by men, so antagonistic to the acceptance of the Four Noble Truths, and so difficult to eradicate, that every effort

[1] *Dham.*, 46, 277. [2] *Magha Sutta*, 575.

should be concentrated on its destruction. Its presence in the mind, however subtle in form, made escape from the changes and attendant suffering of life an impossibility.

Future Existences

THE reign of Ignorance in the mind in regard to the real character of existence entailed a series of numberless successive lives in some form until the difficult lesson could be learned, and escape from its condition be effected through an acquirement of the knowledge of the Four Noble Truths. The doctrine of transmigration was the theory by which the solution of the problem of evil and its attendant condition of suffering in this world was attempted. Present evil existence was the result of evil in a preceding existence. Future existences would be full of happiness or full of sorrow according to the character of this present life. Here was the explanation of the anomalies, wrongs, and evils, as well as of the happiness, prosperity, and blessings so unequally distributed among men. There is something revolting to a Christian in this weary round of interminable existences, from which no man can escape until, after an incalculable amount of almost endless sorrow, he becomes "knowledge-freed," and grasps the principle that suffering is the inevitable attribute of existence. The impossibility of escape is thus graphically described: "Not in the sky, not in the midst of the sea, not if we enter into the clefts of the mountains, is there known a spot in the whole world where a man might be freed from an evil deed."[1] In the Matakabhatta Jātaka there is an illustration of the inexorable succession of rebirths, succeeded by violent deaths five hundred times, as retribution for the one act of taking life. No escape from punishment for that one act was possible until the full tale of transmigrations completed the expiation required.

The great cause of transmigration is Karma. Karma primarily means "act," but as a Buddhist term means "act-force," for the idea is that as a sentient being dies, Karma, the resultant force of all his past actions, brings into existence a new being whose state is happy or miserable, accord-

[1] *Dham.*, 127.

ing to the desert, good or evil, embodied in that resultant force. In an interview with Gotama, a young Brahman said: "From some cause or other mankind receive existence; but there are some persons who are exalted, others who are mean; some who die young, others who live to a great age; some who suffer from various diseases, others who have no sickness until they die; . . . some who are of mean birth, others who belong to the highest caste. What is the cause of these differences? What is it that appoints or controls these discrepancies?" To which Buddha replied: "All sentient beings have their own individual Karma, or the most essential property of all beings is their Karma; Karma comes by inheritance, not from parentage,[1] but from previous births; Karma is the cause of all good and evil. . . It is the difference in the Karma that causes the difference in the lots of men, so that some are mean and others are exalted, some are miserable and others happy."[2] This is an insoluble mystery. It is certainly not fate, for fate overrides the law that effects are the outcome

[1] There is no law of heredity in Buddhism.
[2] Hardy, pp. 445, 446.

of causes. Karma is an effort to find a moral cause for the inequalities of life. It points to a moral and not a physical necessity regulating the nature of life in all sentient beings; as we have already seen it regulates the advent of successive universes. Probably Gotama regarded all action of one sentient being as seed sown, and while that being reaped a partial fruitage from it in this world, much of the seed made up of good and bad elements, remained to spring forth at his death and bear fruit in the existence of a new being, whose place of living, condition, and character were to be determined by it.

The Skandhas of one being pass away and through his Karma, the Skandhas of a new being appear by means of a new birth into some world. The being that died is not reborn, but another person is born who bears the results of guilt, or enjoys the blessings arising from the merit, of the being who died. In other words, there is no continuity of identity. Here is a difficulty, for we should naturally expect that every moral idea would have demanded the continuity of personal identity, when such an act-force was to determine another existence. But there is no "soul" in the Buddhist system and, notwithstanding any popular desire, there is no actual identity of any kind between the two sentient beings that the action of Karma connects, except perhaps the relation which the seed has between the plant that produced it and the plant that it produces. Even here the analogy is only partial. Still Buddha always seemed to imply a very intimate connection between the two beings joined by Karma. "The virtuous man delights in this world and he delights in the next, he delights in both. . . The evil-doer suffers in this world, and he suffers in the next; he suffers in both."[1] Were it not for the positive teaching of non-identity in the absence of a soul, one would feel that transmigration through the influence of Karma was one of souls.

To reconcile the inconsistent principles in these Buddhist doctrines is an impossibility. One can only accept the statements of them. There are no other doctrines that have been such permanent and influential factors in the common daily life of Buddhists. Karma enters into all

[1] *Dham.*, 16, 17.

their thoughts and actions, as an explanation of all the phenomena that attend their lives. The securing of a good Karma by the prescribed offerings of their religion is more active as an influential motive than all the moral precepts. The tendency is to ignore the latter, and offset the want of obedience to them by " gifts " that are supposed to secure a good Karma or " merit." The effort is to obtain that knowledge that dispels ignorance, that perception of misery as the characteristic of all sentient beings, which leads to earnest efforts to realize the benefits of the Eightfold Path in deliverance from transmigration, that *flood* (*ogha*) by crossing which one reaches the island of Nirvāna, that *ocean* (*samudia*) of Sainsāra, whose tossing birth-waves carry one hither and thither, until at last, he who has become an Arhat reaches " the farther shore " and has passed forever beyond existence with its inherent suffering.

The contrast with Christianity is profound. Christianity teaches that man has a soul that should make the best of its existence, not by considering its existence an evil thing because suffering attends it, but by sorrow and penitence for past transgressions, by a noble struggle with the evil within and without himself, and by making the very suffering that he experiences an aid in developing a truly upright character, harmonious with the character of God. By this life, through the divine forgiveness and assistance promised, the guilt of past transgressions is removed and the soul enters not upon fresh probationary existences, but into the fixed, eternal state of the blessed. The Christian Karma, if I may so speak, acts along the line of a continuous personal identity, and there comes to him a conscious experience of the fruit of his former life in the glory of the new one.

The Doctrine of Sin

BUDDHISM does not contain any such doctrinal idea as the Christian idea of sin. Gotama had no true conception of sin as an offense against God, by the transgression of his holy will, for he knew no God. His idea of holiness as perfect conformity to God's perfect law, was equally defective. His morality knew nothing of motives based on the love and fear of God, or based on sin as action contrary to the will of God. His thoughts never rose above the level of humanity in all his teaching. His doctrine is that evil is inherent in the nature of all things that exist, for there is no real soul even in men, hence it is inevitably productive of suffering and demerit, and when he spoke of a good act he referred to an act that would help men to emancipate themselves from suffering and to obtain merit. Therefore, when he exhorted men to good deeds and purity of thought it was not from any idea of overcoming sin in the Christian sense, but to get rid of the demerit of evil actions, and to store up merit by good actions, and thus advance toward that perfection that would bring deliverance from the pain and suffering of all existence. It is because this is forgotten that, looking superficially at his ethical doctrine with its terms so similar in form, and yet so often different in meaning from the terms in Christian ethics, many men frequently either do not see or fail to remember the radically unlike basis on which the Buddhist and Christian systems rest, and exalt Buddhism to an equal if not superior position to Christianity.

Kilesa, depravity, dwells in all forms of existence with its accompanying evil, akusala, demerit. There are ten kinds of Kilesa, viz.: (1) Lobha, desire or cupidity; (2) doso, hate; (3) moho, ignorance or folly; (4) mano, pride; (5) ditthi, heresy; (6) vicikiccha, doubt; (7) thina, sloth; (8) uddhacca, arrogance; (9) ahirika, shamelessness; (10) anotlappa, absence of fear of sinning. These tendencies exist in the very condition of things, and yielding to their influence shows itself in acts which harm the doer by heaping up demerit and forming a hindrance to his progress towards the sanctification of Arhatship. The teachings of the Dhammapada are very explicit: "If a man commits a sin, let him not do it again; let him not delight in sin; pain is the outcome of evil." "Let no man think lightly of evil, saying in his heart, 'It will not come nigh unto me.' Even by the falling of water-drops a water-pot is filled; the fool becomes full of evil, even if he gathers it little by little" (117, 120). The Sucilomasutta[1] teaches that sin originates in the body. "Buddha said, Passion and hatred have their origin from this (body),

[1] 270 *Sut. Nip.*, II., 5.

disgust, delight, and horror arise from this body; arising from this (body) doubts vex the mind, as boys vex a crow." Here the root of sin is not in a mind as the thing tempted and tried, but in the body which is the home of the mind. The description of the body in the Vijaya Sutta, where it is pictured as a contemptible thing, is based on the idea that it is the originator of sin, and that it is not only the prison-house of the mind, but an active enemy, because it is the embodiment of existence with its inevitable evils.

There are several classifications of the principles of sin, and in them some of the principles are repeated. They are:

I. The Ten Precepts, which as prohibitions are directed against certain sinful or improper acts.

II. The Three Âsavas or Defilements. 1. Kamāsava, the lust of the flesh. 2. Bhavāsava, the love of existence. 3. Avijjāsava, ignorance. Sometimes a fourth àsava is added—ditthāsava, the defilement of heresy.

III. The Ten Fetters (dasavidha-samyojana). 1. Sakkāyaditthi, heresy of individuality, *i. e.*, the delusion of believing in a personal self. 2. Vici kiccha, doubt, *i. e.*, of the truth of Buddhist doctrine. 3. Silabbata-paramasa, dependence on ceremonial practices. 4. Kama, lust, bodily passions. 5. Patigha, anger, ill-feeling. 6. Rūparāga, desire for life in natural form (in this or higher worlds). 7. Arāiparāga, desire for life in immaterial form (in the highest heavens). 8. Māna, pride. 9. Uddhacca, exalted judgment of self. 10. Avijja, ignorance.

Perhaps no elements occupy so prominently a place as avijjā, ignorance, tanhā, thirst or desire, and upādāna, clinging (to existence). Ignorance is not a passive, negative thing, the failure to know rightly the great, fundamental teachings of the Four Noble Truths, but it is an active force regnant in a man's life and productive of constant evil. So long as it exists, a man is entangled in the toils of existence and inevitably performs sinful acts, with their sorrowful results. "But there is a taint worse than all taints—ignorance is the greatest taint. O mendicants, throw off that taint and become taintless!"[1]

Tanha, thirst or desire, is an intensely

[1] *Dham.*, 243.

active force in the production of sinful acts. Its importance is shown, not only from the place that it occupies in the Four Noble Truths as the cause of suffering, and in the classification of evil principles, but from the fact that there are at least three sets of Tanhās, each set containing, with some repetitions, three kinds of tanhā, and one set containing six kinds of tanhā. The following passages point out its power over men: "Men, driven on by thirst, run about like a snared hare; held in fetters and bonds, they undergo pain for a long time, again and again. Men, driven on by thirst, run about like a snared hare; let, therefore, the mendicant drive out thirst, by striving after passionlessness for himself."[1] "Those whose wishes are their motives, who are linked to the pleasures of the world, they are difficult to liberate, for they cannot be liberated by others, looking for what is after or what is before, coveting these and former sensual pleasures."[2] The persistence of the power and development of tanhā is compared to the Bīrana grass, that is a pest to the industrious tiller of the soil, for it spreads rapidly

[1] *Dham.*, 342, 343.
[2] *Guhatthakasutta*, 773. *B. E. X.*, p. 177.

and roots deeply into the ground, so that, when he thinks that he has rooted it up, it springs up again with a rapid growth. "Whomsoever this fierce thirst overcomes, full of poison, in this world, his sufferings increase like the abounding Bīrana grass." "This salutary word I tell you, Do ye, as many as are here assembled, dig up the root of thirst as he who wants the sweet-scented Usīra root must dig up the Bīrana grass, that Māra (the tempter) may not crush you again and again as the stream crushes the reeds."[1]

Of the several threefold aspects of tanhā, the desire for sensual pleasure, the gratification of the craving of the senses, is the one that leads to the most practical moral treatment in the ethics of Buddhism. It so weaves itself into the daily life of men, and is so universally successful in bringing misery through the production of sinful acts, that the most forcible presentation of its character and the strongest warnings of the danger, are used to move men to strive to crush it out of their lives. "Subdue thy greediness for sensual pleasures, O Jata kannin," so said the Blessed One;

[1] *Dham.*, 335, 337.

"having considered the forsaking of the world as happiness, let there be not anything either grasped after or rejected by thee." [1]

"Let one wholly subdue the desire of grasping (after everything), O Bhadrāvudha! so said Bhaganat, above, below, across, and in the middle; for whatever they grasp after in the world, just by that Mara follows the man." [2]

Another of the aspects of tanhā, somewhat metaphysical in character, is upādāna, clinging to existence. The sensual desires are but one manifestation of the wish to keep a grasp on things; for below the surface at the root of being, are innate longings for existence often held unconsciously. The connection of this with other aspects of tanhā is not very clear, but perhaps may be explained thus: The second Noble Truth declares that all desire leads to existence. It perpetuates birth after birth. If there were no contact with external things, no contact of the six senses, there would be no grasping after external things, and so there would be no desire for personal exist-

[1] *Jatukanninmanava Puccha,* 1907, *Sut. Nip.,* V., 12.

[2] *Bhadravudhamanava puccha,* 1102.

ence in this or other worlds. The clinging to existence, whether here or hereafter, is a basis of sin, "a source of sorrow." "I see in the world this trembling race given to desire for existences; they are wretched men who lament in the mouth of death, not being free from the desire for reiterated existences."[1] "When he is touched by the touch (of illness) let the Bhikkhu not lament, and let him not wish for existence anywhere, and let him not tremble at dangers."[2]

"And he is a wise and accomplished man in this world; having abandoned this cleaving to reiterated existence he is without desire, free from woe, free from longing, he has crossed over birth and old age, so I say."[3]

The man who has conquered ignorance, desire, and clinging to existence can say: "I have conquered all, I know all, in all conditions of life I am free from taint; I have left all, and through the destruction of thirst, I am free; having learnt myself, whom shall I teach?"[4]

[1] *Kama sutta*, 776; *Sut. Nip.*, IV., 1.
[2] *Tuvataka sutta*, 923; *Sut. Nip.*, IV., 14.
[3] *Mettagumanava puccha*, 1059; *Sut. Nip.*, V., 5.
[4] *Dham.*, 353.

From all these statements the wide distance that separates the basal ideas of sin and sinful acts in Buddhism and in Christianity becomes very plain, and prepares the way for the consideration of the doctrine of "salvation." As two diverging geometrical lines advance with an evergrowing distance, so the Buddhist and Christian ideas of salvation have even a greater divergence than their ideas of sin.

Salvation

THE term salvation means to the Christian, rescue from sin and its penalty, through Divine forgiveness, and a restoration to a life of holy harmony with God that shall be everlasting. To the Buddhist it conveys no such meaning. It only suggests an escape from existence, which is regarded as inherently full of evil and suffering, and being lost in the extinction of Nirvāna.

There is no place for the forgiveness of sins in the Buddhist system, for there is no God of infinite power and love. Consequently there can be no Saviour in the sense that Christ is a Saviour, although one of the favorite appellations given to Gotama is that of saviour.

There is no possible deliverance from the sins arising out of the evil condition that belongs to the body, the dwelling-place of man's mind. Their punishment comes with an unerring certainty. "All that we are, is the result of what we have thought; it is founded on our thoughts, it is made up of our thoughts. If a man speaks or acts with an evil thought, pain follows him as the wheel follows the foot of the ox that draws the carriage."[1]

Inexorable law occupies the place of God in Gotama's system, and the lives and destinies of men are under its dominion. Forgiveness is an impossibility, and the constant burden of the sacred books is the certainty of suffering the penalty of evil deeds. Retribution in one's own self is a theme dwelt on in ghastly materialistic pictures of torments in hells which, after all, have only a temporary part in the application of punishment for evil deeds done, successive rebirths being necessary to complete the expiation. Buddha himself disclaimed any power to deliver men from the

[1] *Dham.*, I.

presence or power of sin, or from its penalty. By his doctrine of Karma, he declared men to be bound to the inevitable consequences of their own transgressions, and the evil actions of the present and former existences avenged themselves in the ills and sufferings of countless subsequent existences. The salvation of Buddha, therefore, can have nothing fundamentally in common with that of Christianity.

1. What is the salvation of Buddhism? In Christianity it is the gift of God to men through the grace of Christ. It involves a great spiritual change, which is the necessary accompaniment of the reception of the forgiveness of sins, and by which a man is prepared for a sinless life in God's presence. In Buddhism salvation is purely intellectual, as is indicated by the derivation of the name Buddhism from *budh,* to know. It was by a perfect enlightenment of the mind, a mental and not a spiritual condition, that the Four Noble Truths were fully apprehended, and a man passed to "the further shore" beyond the ocean of Samsāra to the unconscious calm of non-existence in Nirvāna. "He who takes refuge in Buddha, the Law, and the Sangha, he

who with clear understanding sees the Four Noble Truths, viz., suffering, the origin of suffering, the destruction of suffering, and the Eightfold Path that leads to the quieting of suffering: that is the safe refuge; that is the best refuge; having gone to that refuge, a man is delivered from all pain."

2. By whom is salvation wrought? In Christianity it is wrought by the Saviour, Christ, through his mediatorial life, sufferings, and death. It is wrought outside of men by the God-man with the distinct declaration of the perfect inability of man to do anything to effect his own salvation. But the salvation of Buddhism is a self-wrought thing. The Dhammapada says, "By one's self the evil is done, by one's self one suffers, by one's self evil is left undone, by one's self one is purified. Purity and impurity belong to one's self, no one can purify another" (165). "Well-makers lead the water (wherever they like); fletchers bend the arrow; carpenters bend a log of wood; good people fashion themselves" (145). "Self is the lord of self, who else could be the lord? With self well subdued, a man finds a lord such as few can find" (160). "Not to commit any sin, to do

good, and to purify one's mind, that is the teaching of the Buddha" (183). "Those who are ever watchful, who study day and night, and who strive after Nirvāna, their passions will come to an end" (226).

If we turn to the event of Gotama's attainment of Buddhahood under the Bo Tree (*Ficus Religiosa*) we find that he claimed to have arrived unaided at perfect insight into the nature and cause of sorrow and the method by which it might be destroyed. He had become Buddha, the Enlightened One. He was very clear in the assertion that man must be his own Saviour. By the roadside, on his way to Benares, he met Upaka and answered the inquiry, "Who is your teacher?" with the reply, "I follow no teacher. I have overcome all foes and all stains. I am superior to all men and to all gods; I am the absolute Buddha (Sambuddha). . . . I am the Conqueror."[1] In the Maha-parinibbana Sutta, we are told that three months before his death, Gotama, feeling that his end was near, said to Ananda, "I too am now grown old and full of years, my journey is drawing to a close. I have reached my sum of days. I am turning

[1] *Mahanagga S. B. E.,* XIII.

eighty years of age. And just as a worn-out cart can only with much additional care be made to move along, so, methinks, the body of the Tathāgata can only be kept going with much additional care. When the Tathāgata by abstraction from all marks of outward objects, by extinction of certain sensations, lives in the attainment of that freedom of mind which consists in noting nothing, then only is the Tathāgata's body kept at ease. Therefore, I say, Ananda, be ye lamps unto yourselves. Be ye a refuge to yourselves. Betake yourselves to no external refuge. Hold fast to the truth as a lamp. Hold fast as a refuge to the truth. Look not for refuge to any one besides yourselves."

In a conversation with Ananda at another time, the statement was made that all previous Buddhas had, by their own efforts, passed through the same active training of themselves, and the same personal destruction of lust as Gotama himself.

Thus we see that Buddha did not claim, as Christ did, to be sent by any superior divine power into this world to effect the emancipation of men, but whatever he accomplished was by his own unaided effort through the force of his own meritorious acts after innumerable births in the form of animals, demons, men, and gods. He was the bearer of no supernatural revelation. All that he claimed was to unveil to men the illumination of his mind, accomplished by intense meditation and the severest discipline protracted through cycles of transmigration. He reached salvation, but others could attain the same salvation only by their own individual efforts.

3. How is man to work out his salvation? One great principle may be laid down. A man having withdrawn from the world to a solitary life, having abandoned home for homelessness, pursuing only "right action," must abandon himself to the exercise of intense self-concentration and examination, and to profound abstract meditation until the Great Enlightenment should break upon him.

The keeping of the Ten Precepts lies at the very entrance of a religious life. These, as we have seen, are prohibitions dealing with external life, and lack the wonderful spiritual inwardness of the teachings of Christ on some of the same subjects in the Sermon on the Mount.

But in his enunciation of the Four Noble Truths, Gotama declared the treading of the Eightfold Path (*atthavigako maggo*) to be the way of living that leads to the extinction of suffering. The Path embraces (see p. 101) right belief, right feelings, right speech, right action, right livelihood, right endeavor, right memory, and right meditation. The Dhammapada says: "The best of ways is the eightfold; the best of truths, the four words; the best of virtues, passionlessness; the best of men, he who has eyes to see. This is the way, there is no other that leads to the purifying of intelligence" (273-274). There are beautiful conceptions in this Eightfold Path, and Rhys Davids truly says of it: "He thought that he had discovered a 'Path' which he called 'Noble,' an epithet it most assuredly deserved. Never in the whole history of the world has the bare and barren tree of metaphysical inquiry put forth, where one would least expect it, a more lovely flower—the flower that grew into the fruit which gives the nectar of Nirvāna."[1]

The discussion of these eight divisions of the Noble Path in the Pitakas is more des-

[1] *Bud.*, p. 124.

ultory than one would expect in the case of so prominent a doctrine as the Fourth Noble Truth. " Right belief " is the knowledge of the great principles embodied in Buddha's doctrine of the Four Noble Truths concerning the character of existence, and the path of escape from it. " Right resolution " is acting on this knowledge by withdrawing from the world and showing a humble, kindly behavior. " Right speech " is refraining from lying, slander, abuse, and chattering. " Right conduct " is the avoiding of the taking of life, stealing, and sexual intercourse. " Right livelihood " is the mode of living like a monk, which does not involve the taking of life. " Right exertion " seeks four things, the destruction of demerit which has been acquired, the shunning of the acquirement of demerit in the future, the getting of new merit, and the increase of merit. " Right memory (or mindfulness)" is the constant keeping in mind the real character of the body, the emotions, and the mind. " Right meditation " is the tranquil, trance-like concentration of the mind according to the four-fold method of Jhāna.

Four, at least, of the Pānca sila, that part

of the Dasa sila obligatory on the laity (gahapati) are embodied in these eight divisions.

The last division, right meditation, is the culmination of the beautiful Eightfold Path. It is the grand completion of the system, for it proclaims the need of an inward purity and holiness of life before man can attain Nirvāna, the highest goal of Buddhism. It consists of four stages of sanctification. The means by which one may advance along these stages is Jhāna, a profound absorption in mystic meditation of which there are also four stages. It is in the course of advancement along these four stages of sanctification that the Ten Fetters (dasa sainyejana), already mentioned, are broken.

The first stage of sanctification in the eight divisions of the Eightfold Path is emancipation from the first three fetters, viz., from delusion of self, from doubts about Buddha and his doctrines, and from belief in the power of external rites. The Dhammapada thus describes the excellence of this stage: "Better than sovereignty over the earth, better than going to heaven, better than lordship over all worlds, is the reward of the first step in holiness" (178). The man who has gained this stage of sanctification is called a Sotāpanno, "one who has entered the stream" that will certainly bear him along through whatever existences may remain to him, to the tranquil sea of Nirvāna."

In the first stage of Jhāna, by which this first stage of sanctification is reached, a man secludes himself, and full of the spirit of reflection, fixes his thinking faculties on some particular object until a state of ecstatic joy and serenity is produced. The Sotāpanno may be reborn only in the world of men or in one of the higher worlds.

The second stage of sanctification is emancipation, not only from the first three fetters, but the reduction of sensuality and hatred to such a degree that the person will be reborn in this world only once more. The man who has gained this stage of sanctification is called Sakadāgāmi, "one returning once (to this world)."

In the second stage of Jhāna, by which this second stage of sanctification is reached, a man has such a profound concentration of the mind that the action of the thinking faculties ceases, and only ecstatic joy and serenity remain. The Sakadāgāmi has two existences left, of which one must be passed in this world.

The third stage of sanctification is entire emancipation from the first five fetters, not a trace of low desire for self or toward others remaining. The man who has gained this stage of sanctification is called Anāgami, "one who will not return (to this world)."

In the third stage of Jhāna, by which the third stage of sanctification is reached, only perfect serenity remains. The Anagami has only one existence left to him in a *rūpa brahma loka.*

The fourth stage of sanctification is complete emancipation (Arhattani), in which the mind, purified and exalted, is without any emotion of pain or pleasure. The Ten Fetters are completely broken. Having no longer any bond attaching him to existence and being thereby freed from the power of Karma, at death he will experience no rebirth. He is an Arhat, "a worthy one."

In the fourth stage of Jhāna, by which Arhatship is reached, serenity ceases to exist. There is no movement of thought, no consciousness of joy or sorrow. The Ten

Fetters having been completely broken, the Arhat becomes completely indifferent to all things, good or evil, and dwells in a rapt trance-like state of ecstasy.

Thus we see the processes by which a man, slowly dropping off the impurities and evils of existence, becoming more and more freed from all illusion about the character of its phenomena, advancing in moral holiness, at last arrives at a complete disentanglement from the web of Karma, and enters upon a state of supernatural ecstatic tranquillity, undisturbed by any of the attributes which we consider a necessary part of existence. This is one form of Samādhi, tranquillity, an obscure term which, although it accompanies Jhāna, has also a broader application.

The account of the close of Gotama's life represents that he passed through the four stages of Jhāna, which are also classed as the four of the Eight Attainments (Samappāti). He is also represented as proceeding thence onward to the remaining four attainments, viz.: to the state of the apprehension of infinite space, to that of infinite intelligence, to that of perceiving the nothingness of all things, and to that which is devoid of all consciousness and unconsciousness. Thence he reached Parinirvana.

I have rehearsed the steps in the path of salvation in wearisome detail, in order that there might be as full and fair a representation of the subject as possible. It will be seen that the great principles which run through the Buddhist and Christian systems are widely separated and often antagonistic, and the results sought entirely different, especially the great result, as we shall see in the discussion concerning Nirvāna.

I wish, however, to note here one important differencc between the two systems. The law of salvation by a self-wrought merit is regnant in Buddhism. It is the very essence of the system. On the contrary, in Christianity man is represented as sinful in nature, having no merit of his own, but dependent on the merits of Christ for salvation, his own good works being only a token of his union by faith with Christ in a received divine life. This doctrine of merit is perhaps the doctrine of widest influence among ordinary Buddhists, and often overshadows the influence of the ethical system. The Dhammapada says, "He whose evil deeds are covered by good deeds brightens up this world like the moon when freed from clouds" (173). These good deeds do not necessarily involve any good intention towards others. They may be mere external acts according to the letter of the law, like offerings of flowers at a pagoda, whose sole purpose is to accumulate merit. From a study of Buddhism I feel sure that there are traces of an underlying doctrine of right intention in all acts, that is lost sight of by a large number of its adherents. Men knowingly and deliberately do many things which are wrong and bring demerit, and console themselves by making offerings which they consider will bring merit. They thus deliberately balance Kusala and Akusala against each other, the moral quality of action being completely ignored. When the matter is discussed even by educated natives, an appeal is made to the doctrine of almsgiving as the seed sown in the world about them, especially in the region of monkhood, where it is supposable that moral attainments have been made. All this "liberality" is sure, they believe, to produce merit that will improve their Karma and so benefit them in the next birth. The cause of such a perversion of the law of Kusala must be sought in the innate love which so many men have for their own crooked way, and the effort to offset the results of that way by the outward forms of religion. Thus, by leaving out the moral principle in "good action," Kusala, the very result of Buddhism's own method of salvation by works, is perverted and made a reason for mere external "liberality." It thereby loses the real character which Buddha evidently intended that it should possess.

THE highest attainment, the *summum bonum* which Buddhism holds out to its followers, is Nirvāna. The term is derived from *nir* "not" and *vā* "to blow," and has caused earnest discussion among the students of Buddhism. The word was borrowed from Brahmanism, where it meant the cessation of individual soul-life by its reabsorption into Brahm, the World-Spirit.

Nirvana

Gotama, however, rejected the idea of a soul as well as a supreme World-Spirit. The difficulty of defining the term, as used by Gotama, arises from the fact that it seems to be used in two sets of expressions. In one it sets forth a blissful freedom from human passion and desire; in the other it implies the actual cessation of existence, or at least virtual annihilation. In the former case it applies to Arhats, to whom the term Nirvāna in the Dhammapada exclusively refers. In the latter case it is used with reference to Arhats or a Buddha, after their death.[1] I do not think that there is any clashing of the five applications of the word. When we consider the general trend of Buddhist doctrine, the second application follows naturally out of the first.

1. The term as used with reference to Arhats denotes a state of complete calm that belongs to the final stage of perfect sanctification, and arises from having broken the Ten Fetters.

In the Dhamja Sutta (31)[2] Dhamja declares, "Both my wife and myself are obedient; if we lead a holy life before Sugate, we shall conquer birth and death, and put an end to pain." The Dhamma-

[1] See Childers', Max Müller's, and D'Alives' "Buddhist Nirvana."

[2] *Sut. Nip.*, I., 2.

pada says, "Some people are born again; evil-doers go to hell; righteous people go to heaven; those who are free from all worldly desires attain Nirvāna" (126). The two verses [1] to which Buddhists cling as a joyful utterance by Gotama on his attainment of Buddhahood (Hardy's Manual, p. 180), give the same idea of the extinction of all desire—"Looking for the maker of this tabernacle, I shall have to run through a course of many births, so long as I do not find (him): and painful is birth again and again. But now, maker of the tabernacle, thou hast been seen; thou shalt

[1] 153. Aneka jatisanisaram sandhavissain ambhisain gahakarain gavesanto: dukkha jati punappunain. Gahakaraka ditthosi: puna gehain na kahasi: sabba tephasuka bhagga: gahakutain visankhatain; visankharagatain cittain: tanhanain khayamajjhaga.

The translation in the text is from S. B. E., Vol. X., *Dham.*, 153, 154, but I do not like it, though my opinion may not be of much value. There is much diversity in the translation of the passage. *Sandhavissain,* from *sandhavati,* is taken as a future by Max Müller, a conditional by Fausboll, and an aorist by Childers. I incline to the view of Childers and should prefer some such translation as this, "I ran through several (*i. e.,* many) birth transmigrations, seeking the builder of (this) house, but not finding (him); repeated births are miserable. O housebuilder, thou hast been seen: thou shalt not build the house again; all thy rafters are broken; the ridge-pole is destroyed; the mind is destroyed; it has attained the extinction of desires."

not make up this tabernacle again. All thy rafters are broken, thy ridge-pole is sundered; the mind approaching the Eternal (visankhāra, nirvāna) has attained to the extinction of all desires." The term, in the use of it, means the destruction of kilesa (depravity), tanhā (desire), with its accompanying upādāna (clinging to existence), which through the action of Karma lead to new births and existences. It includes the cessation of all mental action and a state of rapt beatitude in sublime abstraction from self and the outer world. All this is done by the absolute conquest of self through the eradication of self-will, self-assertion, self-seeking, and self-pleasing. The result is a moral condition of sinless, tranquil existence, released forever from all suffering and from all ignorance. This is the Arhat state which Gotama attained at the moment of arriving at Buddhahood, and in this state of Nirvāna he lived until his death.

2. The term is also used to signify cessation of individual existence, a complete end of the series of conscious bodily organizations. There are Buddhists who, under the influence of metaphysical thought, conceive

Nirvāna to be a kind of unconscious existence, an ideal existence in which the mind, having vanquished desire, and destroyed the elements of physical life, knows nothing and feels nothing. This is virtual annihilation and can be only metaphysically conceived as different from absolute annihilation. It is a distinction without any real difference. The term Pari-nirvāna may be used in this connection, for it is only employed to denote skandha-nirvāna, the destruction of the elements of being, which in the death of an Arhat really means the annihilation of existence. At Kūtāgāra, three months before his death, Gotama addressed an assembly of monks, and after reviewing the main points of his doctrine, closed his address with the words, "Behold now, monks, I impress it upon you; all things are subject to the law of dissolution; press on earnestly to perfection; soon the Tathagata's final extinction will take place; at the end of three months the Tāthāgata will enter on final extinction." The Brahmajala sutta seems to give the same idea of extinction. "When the stalk to which a bunch of mangoes is united is cut off, all the mangoes united to that stalk accompany it; even so, monks, the body of Tāthāgata, whose stalk of existence is entirely cut off, still remains; and so long as that body remains, he will be seen by gods and men; but upon the termination of life, when the body is broken up, gods and men shall not see him."[1] In the questions of King Milinda, in reply to the king, who says that if the Buddha accepts gifts, he cannot have entirely passed away, Nagasena declared, "The Blessed One, O king, is entirely set free, and the Blessed One accepts no gift; even at the foot of the Tree of Wisdom, he abandoned all accepting of gifts; how much more then now when he has passed entirely away, by that kind of passing away which leaves no root over (for the formation of a new existence)." Nagasena furnishes illustrations of his idea of the completeness of the Buddha's passing away, comparing him to a fire that has gone out, a wind that has stopped blowing, the sound of a drum that has become silent. All these quotations seem to point to the annihilation of existence at the death of Buddha, or of an Arhat, who shares the same conditions of Nirvāna as a living Buddha.

[1] Quoted by D'Alives, "Nirvana," p. 57.

There is no real contradiction in the two uses of the term Nirvāna. The idea of extinction underlies both. In the first use there is extinction of all those states, tanhā, kilesa, upādāna, with their accompanying evils, attended by the blissful calm resulting from their absence. Nothing remains but the Skandhas (or upādhi), on whose dissolution there is a cessation of existence, as there is no further cause to give rise to new Skandhas. The two ideas of Nirvāna are thus inseparable, and both are equally the reward of a virtuous life. The Nirvāna of Arhatship must precede Pari-nirvāna, the Nirvāna of the Skandhas or elements of existence, without which there can be no further existence. In the Arhat there is an extinction of sin and suffering by a breaking of the Ten Fetters, so that Karma no longer remains to bring about birth with another existence. Nothing remains to the Arhat but the Skandhas, " the slender film of human life." These are all that are left of the fruit of former sin, and being impermanent, will soon pass away. When death comes and the Skandhas disappear, the Arhat arrives at Pari-nirvāna or Aunpādisesa nirvāna. All the constituents of existence are destroyed. There is no further consciousness, no further existence. There is nothing to be conscious, for Karma, which forms the connecting link between existences, has ceased to be, and so there is no existence to be conscious. What is there left to exist? If there is nothing left to exist, the final Nirvāna, Pari-nirvāna, must be the absolute cessation of existence. In the words of the Ratana Sutta, "They, the wise, are extinguished like this lamp."

The second meaning of Nirvāna, as the extinction of existence, seems to harmonize with Gotama's general characterization of existence. According to his teaching, existence is evil, having its roots in Ignorance and Illusion. Men are to seek freedom from the very things that cause existence. Not only so, there is no definite teaching or even hint of an eternal, purified conscious existence after the death of a Buddha or an Arhat. It seems a legitimate inference that if existence is evil in itself, full Nirvāna would be the absolute cessation of existence. Much as this inference seems to be supported by the general tenor of Gotama's teaching, there is no direct formal statement on the subject in the sacred books.

The contrast between the doctrine of Nirvāna (whether interpreted as extinction or an indefinite, unconscious state of being that seems to me a virtual extinction) and the Christian doctrine of an endless, sinless, blissful life is immense. The Christian doctrine responds to our human love of life and expectation of a life hereafter in its presentation of immortality; the Buddhist doctrine cuts across these human feelings and presents the barren, cheerless prospect of a virtual, if not real extinction as the ultimate goal of a saintly life. It is no wonder that the great body of the common people and even the monks regard Nirvāna as such an inconceivably vast distance away, that they are content to exert themselves, if they do anything, to be reborn in some one of the happy heavens that Buddhism declares to exist.

Still there is a slight parallelism connected with the eternal life of Christianity and the Nirvāna of Buddhism. Both must be obtained in this world, though their complete possession remains to be obtained after death. Both carry with them exemption from the power of death, but in very different senses. The final life of the Christian is immortal, beyond the reach of death, but its beginning is here, for "He that believeth hath life." Nirvāna is not immortality, for immortality involves life; it is the escape of the whole individual beyond the range of real existence, for over any real existence death must have power; but it cannot take place until the preliminary Nirvāna of the Arhatship has been gained here.

Can any one say that the Christian doctrine, allowing the noblest realization of the soul's aspirations, is not immeasurably superior to the Buddhist doctrine that condemns our very existence as something so evil that the oblivion of extinction in nothingness is a blessing?

Conclusion

In this necessarily brief outline of Buddhism compared with Christianity, much that I would like to have discussed has been passed over for want of space. Still, I think that enough has been presented to set forth the fundamental differences between the two great religions and their founders. At the risk of some repetition, it may be well to sum up these differences.

At the very beginning Christ stands before us as a great historical person set forth in the wonderfully simple yet vivid narratives of the Evangelists. Gotama stands before us, a historical person indeed, but with only a few salient events of his life of which we can feel sure, such is the mist of legend that envelops him. The likeness between these two great characters is very distant, while the differences are marked and radical. There is no real similarity in the stories of their birth; in the prophecy of Asita, and the visit of the Magi. There is some similarity in their age at the time of their entrance upon their public ministries, one being about thirty years and the other thirty-five years old, but the length of their ministries was very different. Buddha foretold his death three months before its occurrence. Christ also prophesied his crucifixion before it took place. There are three great epochs in their lives which may be compared—Gotama's entrance on Buddhahood and Christ's recognition by the Holy Spirit at his baptism on the threshold of his ministry; the First Sermon in the deer park at Benares and the Sermon on the Mount near the Sea of Galilee; and the death at Kusī-nagara and that on Calvary. But whatever similarity one may find, the divergences are so great as to obliterate any superficial likeness. For one, I have always failed to see any similarity in the deaths of these two great persons. One died peacefully, surrounded by many disciples, receiving what was, according to his own representation, a final emancipation from existence. The other died in agony at the hands of wicked men, looking upon himself as bearing the sin of the world, in a great and final atoning sacrifice to take his life again in glorious power. The principles which animated their minds in their dying hour were as antagonistic as the opposite poles of a battery.

The methods of instruction employed by Buddha and by Christ have similarity in the frequent use of pithy sayings and of illustrations. In the Dhammapada which Max Müller inclines to think may be considered as containing the utterances of Buddha, there are not a few sayings that resemble the words of Christ in brevity and pointedness of style. "Let a man overcome anger with love; let him overcome evil by good; let him overcome the greedy by liberality; the liar by truth."[1] These words remind one of the command, "Love your enemies, do good to them which hate you,"[2] or of the exhortation of Paul, "Be not overcome of evil, but overcome evil by good." As Gotama says, "Many men whose shoulders are covered by the yellow gown are ill-conditioned and unrestrained, such evil-doers by their evil deeds go to hell."[3] Christ says, "Beware of false prophets which come to you in sheep's clothing, but inwardly they are ravening wolves."[4]

In the use of illustration, however, there is a contrast not only in the subject-matter, but in the form in which illustration is used. The subject-matter follows the great divergence of doctrine in the two faiths. In form, Buddha's illustration appears more in stories, similes, and fables than in proper parables, while parables are most frequently used by Christ. The story of Kisāgotami has been called "The Parable of the Mustard Seed," but it is really a story.

[1] *Dham.*, 223.
[2] Luke 6 : 27.
[3] *Dham.*, 307.
[4] Matt. 7 : 15.

The Kasibharadvajasutta,[1] sometimes called "The Parable of the Sower," comes nearer to the style of a true parable.

The reputed miracles of Gotama are very different in kind and object from those of Christ. They lack any specially moral element, and have no necessary part in Gotama's ministry. In Christ's ministry his miracles are so intimately related to his teachings that miracles and teachings must stand or fall together. His miracles are never worked for display, and always have a benign object. On the other hand, the miracles of Gotama are rather portents than miracles, and seem to be an afterthought wrought into the legends through the ascription of supernatural power to Buddha, such as the miracles attending the conversion of the thousand Jatilas or Fire-Worshipers; the conquering of the poisonous serpent in the temple of the sacred fire; the instantaneous journey to gather fruit from the far-away Jambu tree and the return in the little interval between his command to the Jatila to go in to breakfast and the immediate obedience of the Jatila to the command; and the last miracles, stated to be

[1] *Sut. Nip.*, I., D.

three thousand five hundred in number, when, Buddha wishing to wash his ragged robe, a tante, a stone to beat the clothes on, and other needed things were provided, water came or disappeared as wished, five hundred sticks of wood were split or prevented from being split, and five hundred fires were kindled or not, according to his exercise of supernatural power. The Mahāparinibbana Sutta mentions one miracle. Having come to a river which was overflowing its banks, and wishing to cross, Gotama, as his followers started in search of material for a raft, vanished to the other shore as swiftly as a man can stretch forth his arm. The legendary character of such miracles is stamped upon them.

There was a great difference in the reception that these great teachers received from the people. Gotama made a multitude of disciples, who were mostly men of wealth and position. Christ gathered only a few disciples, who were largely from the poor of the lower ranks of society. Gotama was entertained by kings and nobles, received gifts of parks for residence and abundant offerings of food, and was, as a rule, eagerly sought for as he itinerated. Christ was despised and hated by the ruling powers, lived his life of poverty with only an exceptional kindly notice from the rich and powerful, and though often thronged by curious crowds, was generally received with the spirit of unbelief and rejection.

In the spirit of self-sacrifice that animated Gotama and Christ there is another form of difference. Gotama is represented in the Jātaka stories, as at one time, for the good of others, having plucked out his eyes, and at other times having cut off his head, having chopped himself to pieces, having given up his children, etc. There is only one particular act in the Pitakas that reminds us of any occurrence in the Gospels. As the story runs: A mendicant who had become very ill, was left uncared for by his fellow-mendicants. Buddha told Ananda, "Fetch some water; you and I will bathe this monk." When Ananda had brought the water, Buddha poured it over the sick mendicant, and Ananda wiped him. Then Buddha, lifting the head and Ananda the feet, they placed him on his bed. In this there is a distant resemblance to the story of Christ's washing the disciples' feet. But whatever external resemblance one may think that he discovers, the fundamental principles underlying the self-sacrifice are widely divergent. Buddhism demands a non-selfishness not so much for the good of others as for the repression of self to attain the longed-for knowledge by which ignorance will be dispelled, and the illusion of personal existence disappear. Christianity demands an active self-abnegation for the good of others, by which personal existence may be so elevated and ennobled that in the future state an ideal divine life may be realized.

I have dwelt at length on the comparison of the lives of the founders of these two religions, because there is much in those lives that is the embodiment of their doctrines. After the consideration given to the system of ethics and of doctrines in the body of the essay, there is no need of a further detailed comparison of them. We have seen that the Christian sense of morality as a duty to God finds no place in the Buddhist system. While there are so many moral precepts in common with Christianity, they are enforced on a very different ground—the acting rightly to get rid of suffering, and end the sense of individuality and existence. In its ethical teaching Buddhism makes no use of the emotions as an incentive to a righteous life. It calls on men who truly wish to enter the path of sanctification to abandon the love of home and family, affection for relatives and friends, even active sympathy with the afflicted, and rise into a calm which is unconscious of love, hatred or any other emotion. But Christianity exalts love and makes love to God and love to man the grand motive, as well as fulfilment of right action.

A religion that has no God or Creator, allows no existence of a soul, despises and contemns the body, has no true idea of sin as the transgression of a Divine Will, has no knowledge of how evil first entered the world, looks upon life as only a state of suffering and impermanence through countless transmigrations, offers as the only salvation a final deliverance from existence itself through a self-wrought righteousness in which the demerit of interminable existences is balanced by the slowly gained merit of other interminable existences, Nirvāna, meanwhile, seeming as far away as the end of an arithmetical progression, has little in common doctrinally with Christianity, which puts God as the great source of our being and duty, proclaims the presence of a soul that is the breath of God in us, regards the body as a sacred temple, teaches that sin is the transgression of the known will of the heavenly Father, declares how evil entered the world and its awful consequences to the life of man that is unending in its nature, offers a full and free deliverance from evil and its consequences in the forgiveness of sin through an all-powerful Redeemer, and an immediate entrance upon a perfect, holy state at death.

Like Christianity, Buddhism teaches that its blessings are open to all. The Vasala Sutta[1] very clearly shows that Gotama decried all caste distinctions and taught that there was no "outcast" except the man doing evil deeds: "Not by birth does one become an outcast, not by birth does one become a Brāhmana; by deeds one becomes an outcast, by deeds one becomes a Brāhmana." Practically, however, the fullest blessing is possible only to members of the Sangha. Men as gahapatis may make advance in merit, especially by "liberality" to the Sangha. But, abandoning marriage

[1] *Sut. Nip.*, I., 7.

as after all evil in itself, they must join the Sangha, if they are ever really to enter the path of sanctification. This really shuts out, for the present existence, at least, a multitude of men who are bound by honorable domestic ties. Then certain classes, like lepers, are positively debarred from entering the Sangha, as is shown by the questions put to the candidate at the so-called ordination service for reception into the Sangha. Christianity proclaims as a glorious truth that its blessings of redemption and eternal life are open to all men of whatever character without a single condition, who seek those blessings by faith in Christ.

Buddhism has had its ardent missionary spirit, as well as Christianity, and, as a rule, has not resorted to any violent methods in promulgating its doctrines. The account of Mahinda's missionary life in Ceylon is intensely interesting, and shows the fervor of early Buddhists. But while Buddhism has proved successful in winning its way in former centuries, fostering education and literature, commanding peace, kindly feeling, and brotherhood among men, urging the embodiment of high virtues in daily life and deprecating the many evils that thrive in human society, it has not had a living, sustaining zeal, but has lost its early ardor and has fallen into its present apathetic state. In this it is unlike Christianity, whose missionary zeal was never more vigorous and aggressive than now. Doubtless the secret is in the difference of doctrine and corresponding difference of hope that were in each system. Gotama sent his disciples on their mission and so did Christ, but, after all, the missionary work of the Sangha was a ministry to others, not out of love to Gotama, but with primary reference to self, while the missionary work of the Christian is a service of others through love and obedience to Christ as the primary motive power. Love of God and man is a greater living, inspiring, enduring power for action than love that finds an ultimate end in self. The present atrophy of Buddhist missionary effort is doubtless due to an apathy of feeling which is the real outcome of the trend of its fundamental doctrines after the energy and fervor that accompanied its establishment died out of the hearts of its followers in the passing of centuries.

Another reason may be found in the teaching of Buddha that his doctrine would wax, wane, and disappear at the end of five thousand years. Accepting this as true, and feeling that after the lapse of half that time, the summit of prosperity has been already passed and the wane begun, men are not moved to contend against the inevitable destiny of decay that it has entered upon. This is not a random statement, but is the expressed feeling of monks whom I have met. The hope that the promised triumph of Christianity brings to its followers is not known to Buddhists and its inspiring power is therefore unfelt by them. Urged by that hope, Christians are moved to aggressive effort for the spread of their religion.

Thus Buddhism stands before us with Gotama, a pure, noble, true man, as its founder, and the teacher of the highest system of morality outside the Christian Scriptures. Yet, when we touch the soul's deep needs, its craving for deliverance from the power and the results of sin, its longing for an omnipotent Deliverer by whose assistance it may reach a sinless, happy state, we find in Gotama no answering divine voice that speaks relief. The voice is the voice of a man, thoughtful indeed and versed in the knowledge of the human heart, but still the voice of only a man, offering a cold and dreary philosophy of life, which in its course and result cuts athwart all the intuitions and aspirations of a human soul. He honestly sought to solve the problem of human suffering and escape from it. But a fountain cannot rise above its source, and the system of Gotama is only human and inadequate to its object. Turning to Christianity, we hear a divine voice that responds to every human need, telling of deliverance from sin through a loving, omnipotent Saviour and of the eternal life of heaven. Here is a salvation complete in itself, according with every want of man. Therefore, turning from the "Light of Asia" to the "Light of the World," we accept as truth his declaration, "I am the Way, the Truth, and the Life."

Index